Anglotopia's Dictionary of British English

British Slang from A to Zed

2nd Edition

By Jonathan Thomas

Anglotopia

ALSO BY ANGLOTOPIA

To my lovely wife, Jackie.

Table of Contents

Introduction

It's been almost five years now since we published the 1st edition of Anglotopia's Dictionary of British English. We've been blown away by how popular the book has been and felt that it was time to update the book with more words and some additional articles about British culture.

Many readers bought this book to help them translate what they were watching when they viewed British TV, so many of the additions to the book reflect that.

What really surprised us was how many copies of this book we sold to the UK – almost as many as we did to the USA! It appears Anglotopia's take on these words is popular with the British.

Nothing inspires pedantry quite like the English language and all its various uses and over the years we've gotten quite an earful from people about our definitions and our usage of some words. We've updated this book to reflect words that were wrong or have changed with time.

However, we must first look at the question: What is British English? This has been the biggest criticism (you will not believe the angry letters we get!) because technically there is no such thing as 'British English.' It's just English.

So, how do we separate the English the British speak from what Americans speak? American English is a technical term. You can't call it English English.

Taking into consideration the primary audience for this book, we will continue to call the version of English spoken by the inhabitants of the British Isles British English. They may not like it, but it's the definition that works for Americans.

The second point people wrote us about was that we call so many common words slang, when they aren't slang. This is true. Many words defined in this book are not technically slang. They're just words that are not unusual to the British but are to us.

So then what is British Slang? It's something that doesn't technically exist, as most British people are quick to point out. But this book isn't for them.

We pesky Americans search out and call it British Slang. This is how we define the types of words and how they're used differently in the UK. It may not be technically correct, but it's a similar technicality to us removing extraneous u's from our words. The definition works for this audience and we'll stick with it.

We've also had Americans write to us and take issue with us insisting that some words are British Slang when they've heard the words their whole life. English is a continually evolving language.

Those in the Southern USA may find many of these words familiar, but we in the north may not be familiar with them. Many Canadians may comment that these words aren't slang to them – but Canada has a much closer knit relationship to Britain than we do.

My perspective is as a student of the English language from the Midwest of the USA. So inclusions in this book are based on words that I've come across or seen used in British media. Some words may not be included because they are so common (and we've omitted many from other sources because America and Britain agree they mean the same thing).

Also, readers of the 1st edition found it a bit crass because we included so many vulgar words. They wish they had been warned, so consider this a warning. This book is filled with foul British language and also some very insulting words. We've declined to include some very offensive words but we generally air on the side of caution that you would rather know what it means than not. This is for educational purposes and we certainly don't advocate insulting people.

No longer will you have to scratch your head about the meaning of something. With this dictionary by your side, you'll always have a way to translate from Brit speak to American English.

It was not possible to include every word the British use differently without it becoming an actual dictionary so we've limited the list to more common words and phrases. Most of our definitions are based on comparisons to American English so that's the perspective from which we have written.

We've excluded words that basically have the same meaning in both American and British English and there are a lot of words that were cut because there is no need to be redundant, we wanted this text to be a quick reference.

Other British Slang Dictionaries separate words by category, we dispensed with that and made one master dictionary of all British English words and created several sections exploring distinct dialects of British English (such as Scouse, Yorkshire, West Country, etc).

Enjoy!

Cheers,
Jonathan
Anglophile-in-Chief
Anglotopia

A

AA - *abbr* - The British Automobile Association, whom you call when your car breaks down. Not to be confused with Alcoholics Anonymous.

A&E - *n* - Accident and Emergency, what Americans would call the Emergency Room.

A - Levels - *n* - The highest level of secondary education that culminates in a series of standardized tests.

Abattoir - *n* - A place where an animal is butchered.

Abdabs - *n* - To be scared or frightened of something.

Absobloodylootely - *n* - To agree with someone highly in a rather enthusiastic fashion. Somewhat vulgar.

Ace - *n* - Excellent or wonderful.

Action man - *n* - The equivalent to the U.S. G.I. Joe or a man that does macho things.

Advert - *n* - An advertisement or commercial.

Advocate – *n* – Scottish Barrister.

Aerial - *n* - A television antenna, usually located on the roof, but can also refer to the antenna on the television itself.

Aerodrome – *n* – Airfield or small airport.

Aeroplane - *n* - How the British spell 'airplane'.

Afters - *n* - Another name for the dessert course at dinner.

AGA - *n* - A massive cooking range modeled with a vintage look.

Aggro - *n* - Abbreviation of "aggravation". Something that is rather annoying.

Agony Aunt - *n* - A newspaper advice columnist.

Air Biscuit - *n* - A fart.

Airy-Fairy - *adj* - Someone who is lacking in strength or ability.

Alcopop - *n* - Canned or carbonated fruit drinks with alcohol in them.

Aled up - *adj* - To be drunk as the result of drinking ale.

Alight - *v* - To disembark or get off a mode of transport like a train or bus.

All fur coat and no knickers - *adj* - A woman who looks good on the surface but has no substance.

All Mod Cons - *n* - A home or car with all the modern conveniences.

All mouth and no trousers - *adj* - To be boastful without justification.

All over the Gaff - *n* - To be disorganized.

All over the shop - *adj* - **1.** To be disorganized. **2.** Everywhere

All to pot - *adj* - Something that's gone completely wrong.

Allotment - *n* - A garden plot in a shared community garden.

Alright! - e*xclam* - A simple greeting. It's not a question asking how you are.

Aluminium - *n* - It's just Aluminum.

Amber nectar - *n* - Lager (beer).

Anchors - *n* - Brakes on a car.

Ankle-biters - *adj* - A derogatory term for children.

Anorak - *n* - **1.** A nerd or someone who is geeky about something like a planespotter, trainspotter or Anglophile. **2.** A light waterproof jacket perfect for rambling in the countryside.

Answerphone - *n* - An answering machine. Bit of an outdated term now that voicemail is common.

Anti-clockwise - *adv* - It means the same thing as 'counter clockwise.'

Antenatal - *adj* - Prenatal care.

Appeal – *n* – Fundraising campaign.

Apples and Pears – *n* – Cockney Slang for stairs.

Argue the toss - *v* - To dispute something at length.

Argy-bargy - *n* - Trouble, noisy or having an argument.

Arrows - *n* - Another word for darts, the actual darts themselves, not the game.

Arse - *n* - Buttocks.

Arse about Face - Back to front.

Arse over tip – *inf* – Head over heels.

Arsehole - *n* - An asshole.

Arsemonger - *n* - A person worthy of contempt.

Arse-over-tit - *adj* - To fall over, often as the result of alcohol. To be intoxicated.

Arterial Road – *n* – Main road.

Articulated Lorry – *n* – Tractor trailer semi.

As rare as hen's teeth - *adj* - Something that's rare.

ASBO - *n* - Anti-social behavior order - a punishment on people who repeatedly disturb the peace.

Assizes – *n* – Court sessions.

At risk – *n* – In danger. That whole history building is at risk of being torn down.

Aubergine - *n* - Otherwise known as an eggplant.

Au fait – *inf* – Conversant.

Auntie Beeb – *n* – Affectionate nickname for the BBC.

Aussie kiss - *n* - Oral sex on a woman.

Autocue – *n* - Teleprompter.

Autumn - *n* - The British don't have Fall, they have Autumn, the season that precedes winter.

Axe - *n* - A guitar.

Axe wound - *n* - Vagina.

B

Baby batter - *n* - Semen.

Backhander - *n* - Bribe.

Back bacon – *n* - Canadian bacon.

Back Bench – *n* – Members of Parliament who are not member of the Government and thus sit behind the front benches normally occupied by the Government. A Back Bench MP.

Back passage - *n* - Anus.

Back scuttle - *n* - Anal intercourse.

Badger - *v* - To ask someone something incessantly.

Bad Hat – *inf* – A bad egg.

Bagsie - *v* - Calling dibbs on something. For example, I call bagsies on the front seat of the car.

Bailiff – *n* – 1. Sherrif's assistant. 2. Estate or farm manager.

Bairn - *n* - Another word for baby, usually used in Scotland, but also common in the north of England – particularly in Newcastle.

Baldy notion - *n* - To have an idea or a clue about something.

Ball bag - *n* - Scrotum. Also used as an insult.

Balloon Knot - *n*- The anus.

Ballsed up - *adj* - A situation that's all messed up.

Bally - *n* - Short for Balaclava, a type of mask that covers your face. Also used as a softer version of bloody. e.g. "You bally fool."

Bare - *n* - To say that there is a lot of something.

Baltic - *n* - To describe something as very cold, referring to the Baltic region.

Banger - *n* - Short term for the traditional English sausage. When served with mashed potatoes, it's called bangers and mash.

Bang on - *adj* - Exactly or correct.

Bang out of order - *adj* - Totally unacceptable.

Bank Holiday - *n* - A public holiday in the UK. Usually they don't have any special meaning other than a day off that allows a long weekend. However, Christmas, Boxing Day etc are usually Bank Holidays as well.

Bank Note – *n* –A unit of currency or paper money.

Banter – *v* – Taking the piss out of your friends, making fun of them. There's a fine line between banter and being a jerk. Sometimes its lost on foreigners.

Bap - *n* - A breadroll.

Baps - *n* - Another name for a woman's breasts.

Barge-pole – *n* – A ten foot pole.

Barking - *adj* - Insane or crazy.

Barmpot - *n* - A stupid person that has the added distinction of being clumsy.

Barmy - *adj* - To be crazy or insane.

Barnet - *n* - Another name for human hair, Cockney roots in the location of Barnet.

Barney - *n* - To be in big trouble.

Baronet – *n* – Lowest order of hereditary peerages. Uses the Sir prefix.

Barrister - *n* - A lawyer that practices in front of higher court judges.

Bash on - *interj* - To go on regardless of the problems facing you in a situation.

Basin – *n* – Bathroom sink.

Bathroom Cubicle – *n* – Bathroom stall.

Bathing costume – *n* – Bathing suit.

Bean - *n* - 1. An ecstasy pill 2. The female clitoris.

Bearded clam - *n* - Female genetalia that's covered in pubic hair.

Bearskin – *n* – Hat worn by the soldiers that guard HM The Queen.

Beat the bishop - *v* - To masturbate.

Beavering - *v* - To work industriously at something. Not used as much these days because of what the word 'beaver' means in American English.

Bee's Knees, The - *adj* - Something that is awesome and wonderful.

Bedfordshire - *n* - Bed or bedtime. Said as "I'm off to Bedfordshire."

Bedsit - *n* - An apartment where the bedroom serves as the living space similar to a studio apartment.

Beeb - *n* - Shorthand for the BBC.

Beefeater – *n* – The warder guards of the Tower of London.

Belisha Beacons - *n* - The yellow flashing lights at a pedestrian crossing in the UK.

Bell-end - *n* - The end of the male genetalia. Also an insult to call someone stupid. "Don't be such a bell-end."

Belt – *n* – Girdle.

Belt Up - *interj* - Shut up.

Bender - *n* - 1. An epic alcohol drinking session. 2. A derogatory term for a male homosexual.

Bent - *n* - A derogatory term for a homosexual.

Berk - *n* - An idiot or irritating person.

Bespoke - *adj* - Something that is custom made for you. i.e. bespoke cabinetry.

Best of British - *v* - To wish someone good luck.

Bevvy - *n* - An Alcoholic drink.

Bill, The - *n* - A slang term for the Police. The term was popularized by a British television series of the same name.

Billy no-mates - *n* - A person who doesn't have any friends.

Billy - *n* - Amphetamine drugs.

Bin - *n* - A trashcan.

Bin liner - *n* - A garbage bag that goes in a trashcan.

Bin man - *n* - Garbage man.

Bint - *n* - A derogatory word for woman who is just above a prostitute.

Bird - *pron* - An attractive girl or woman.

Biro - *n* - A ball point pen.

Birthday Honours – *n* – When titles and honours (such as Sir) are given out on the Queen's Birthday.

Biscuit - n - What Americans call a cookie. As a corollary it has nothing to do with what Americans call a biscuit.

Bits and bobs - *n* - Bits and pieces.

Bitter – *n* – Bitter beer. A pint of Bitter.

Blag - *v* - To scam something. Blagging is to pretend to be someone else to steal their personal information or access their bank accounts.

Bleeding - *adj* - Another use of the word bloody. Damned.

Blighter - *adj* - A man or a boy.

Blighty - *n* - An older term that simply means Britain.

Blimey - *interj* - Exclamation similar to "Oh no!" or "Oh dear!" Can also be used to express excitement.

Blinding - *adj* - Something that is uniquely wonderful

Blink - *adj* - Something that's not working. "On the blink."

Blinking - *adj* - Damned.

Bloke - *n* - Guy or man.

Bloody - *adj* - The British equivalent to the word damn and it is considered a mild curse word.

Blooming - *adj* - A much lighter way to say bloody. The American equivalent would be 'darn.'

Blow off - *v* - Fart.

Blower - *n* - Telephone.

Blub - *v* - To cry.

Blue Vinney – *n*- A type of stinky blue cheese made in Dorset.

Boat Race – *n* – Annual boat race on the Thames between Oxford and Cambridge.

Bob - *n* - 5 pence piece (used to be a shilling)

Bob's your uncle - *interj* - There you have it!

Bobbie - *n* - Police officer.

Bobbins - *adj* - Something that's crap.

Bodge - *v* - Something haphazard or cobbled together.

Bodge job - *n* - A poorly done job.

Bodger - *n* - A person who works with wood, a wood turner.

Boff - *v* - To have sexual intercourse.

Boffin - *n* - Policy wonk or someone that is knowledgeable on a subject.

Bog - *n* - The toilet.

Bog roll - *n* - Toilet paper.

Bog standard - *n* - Normal or average.

Bogie - *n pron* - A booger.

Boiler - *n* – 1. A hot water heater. 2. An unkind term for an ugly woman.

Boiler Suit – *n* – Coveralls – a siren suit. Churchill was fond of them.

Bollard - *n* - Metal post that usually indicates a place one should not drive into.

Bollocks - *n* - 1. Male testicles. 2. Something that is rubbish or crap. 3. Exclamation, displaying irritation at an outcome.

Bollocking - *n* - To be punished severely or told off.

Bolshie - *adj* - A rebel.

Bolt-hole - *n* - A hideaway place, usually a country cottage.

Bomb - *n* - A splendid success.

Bonce - *n* - The top of one's head.

Bonfire night - *n* - Also known as Guy Fawkes Day, fireworks and bonfires are usually held to celebrate the capture of Guy Fawkes.

Bonnet - *n* - The hood of a car.

Bonny - *adj* - Scottish for beautiful.

Boot - *n* - The car's trunk, opposite of the bonnet.

Boozer - *n* - A pub or bar.

Boracic - *n* - Without money. From rhyming slang 'Boracic Lint' - Skint.

Borstal – *n* – Reformatory – where Britain's original Juvenile Detention center was.

Bothy – *n* – Hut, small cottage in the wilderness. Originally used by farmers, now can be rented by hikers. Common in Scotland.

Bottle - *n* - To have a lot of nerve. He's got a lot of bottle! Also used as a verb, to denote that someone has lost their nerve, e.g. "he's bottled it."

Bounder - *n* - A useless person.

Boss Eyed – *adj* – Crossed Eyed.

Box - n – 1. A rather rude way to refer to the female genitalia. 2. Also a piece of protective gear worn by cricketers to protect the genitals from being impacted.

Boxing Day - *n* - The day after Christmas. A public holiday where everyone has the day off but doesn't really have any special meaning anymore.

Braces - *n* - Suspenders.

Brackets - *n* - Parentheses. '( )'

Brassed Off - *adj* - To be fed up with something that's frustrating you. Similar to 'pissed off' in American English.

Break wind - *v* - Fart.

Brekky - *n* - Breakfast.

Brew - *n* - A cup of tea.

Brick - *n* - A person that you can rely on.

Bricking it - *v* - Terrified.

Brigadier – *n* – Military rank between colonel and major general.

Brill - *adj* - Short for brilliant!

Brilliant! - *adj* - Exclamation for something that is awesome.

Brolly - *n* - Umbrella.

Broadsheet – *n* – Large sized newspaper.

Brownfield land - *n* - Former industrial land that is available for re-use.

Brush - *n* - A broom.

Brummie – *n* – Someone from Birmingham. The term can also refer to the accent and dialect common to Birmingham.

BSE - Acronym - (Bovine spongiform encephalopathy) - Mad Cow Disease.

BST – *abrv* – British Standard Time.

Bubble and squeak - *n* - Boiled cabbage and sausage.

Buck House – *n* – Shorthand for Buckingham Palace.

Buff - *adj* - Sexually attractive; Also a word for nude, sometimes used loosely to describe the act of sex e.g. "We was buffin' for hours."

Bugger - *n* - An exclamation of dissatisfaction ("Oh bugger!"), in a dire situation ("Well, we're buggered now"), acute surprise ("Well bugger me!"), dismissal ("bugger that").

Buggery - *n* - The act of anal sex.

Builder - *n* - A construction worker or contractor.

Builder's bum - *adj* - Plumber's crack.

Builder's tea - *n* - Strong, inexpensive tea taken by people in the building trade, usually in a mug.

Bum - *n, v* - Buttocks. Not particularly rude - more acceptable in polite circles than 'arse.'

Bum bag - *n*- What Americans would call a fanny pack (don't call it a fanny pack in the UK, see 'fanny'.)

Bum bandit - *n* - Homosexual, derogatory.

Bum cleavage - *n* - The area between the buttocks.

Bumf - *n* - Too much paperwork.

Bung - *n* - To give or throw a game. A bribe.

Bunk off - *v* - To call off sick or not fulfil your duties.

Burgle - *n* - To break into a building.

Busker - *v* - Street musician.

Butcher's - *n* - To look at something.

Butlin's (Also Butlins) – *n* – A chain of family holiday camps.

Butty - *n* - A sandwich usually sold in chip shops that consists of sausages and chips. Or both. Chiefly used in parts of the north of England.

By-election – *n* – A
special election to fill an
empty House of
Commons Seat usually
after a death or
resignation.

C

C of E - *n* - A short way of saying Church of England - England's official state Church.

Cabbage - *n* - 1. Vegetable 2. Someone who is brain-dead or catatonic.

Cack - *n* - Shit.

Cack-handed - *n* - Clumsy or inept.

Caff - *n* - A café.

Cakehole - *n* - Mouth - 'shut your cakehole'

Camp - *adj* - Effeminate or homosexual.

Camper van - *n* - Recreational vehicle.

Candy floss - *n* - Cotton Candy.

Cans - *n* - Headphones.

Capsicum – *n* – Green pepper.

Car boot sale - *n* - Swap meet or flea market where people sell items from the back of their car.

Car park - *n* - Parking lot or parking garage.

Caravan - *n* - Another term for Recreational Vehicle.

Cardie - *n* - Short for cardigan which is a type of sweater.

Care Home – *n* – Nursing home.

Carrier bag - *n* - Shopping bag.

Carry on - *v* - To continue with something.

Carvery – *n* – Buffet restaurant.

Cash Point (or Cash Machine) – *n* – Automated Teller Machine (ATM)

Casualty Department – *n* – The emergency room or the A&E.

Cat's eyes - *n* - Reflectors located on the road in the center line.

Caught-short – *v* – The need to use the bathroom but no having access to a facility to do so.

Central reservation - *n* - The median of the road.

Cesspit – *n* – A septic or wastewaster tank.

Chambermaid – *n* – Hotel maid.

Chancer - *n* - A person willing to take risks or take a chance.

Changing room – *n* – Dressing room.

Chap - *n* - A man, bloke or guy.

Charity Shop – *n* – Thrift store, secondhand store where the proceeds benefit a charity.

Chartered Accountant – *n* – A CPA – Certified Public Accountant.

Chat up - *v* - Trying to pick someone up in a bar or elsewhere.

Chattering Classes - *n* - Snobby upper class people chiming in on something.

Chav - *n* - A derogatory term used towards the lower classes with a similar meaning to 'white trash' but applies to all races.

Chavtastic - *n* - Something that is in poor taste that a Chav would appreciate.

Cheeky - *adj* - Risqué or clever.

Cheerio - *interj* - Goodbye!

Cheers - *interj* - Simply means thank you but it also works as a drinking toast.

Chelp - *v* - To disagree vocally with someone without sufficient grounds to do so.

Chemist - *n* - Pharmacist but it should be noted they can also provide simple medical advice without having to go to a doctor.

Chesterfield - *n* - Hard leather sofa.

Child-minder – *n* – A babysitter, someone who looks after children.

Chinese Whispers - *n* - What Americans would call Chinese Telephone.

Chipolata - *n* - A small sausage.

Chippy - *n* - A fish and chip shop.

Chips - *n* - French Fries, usually thick cut.

Chivvy on - *v* - To hurry along.

Chock-a-block - *adj* - Closely packed together i.e. a busy schedule.

Chocolate box - *adj* - Excessively decorative and sentimental, like the old pictures on boxes of candy. Usually used to describe a quaint village.

Chocolate drops - *n* - Chocolate chips.

Christmas Cracker - *n* - A Christmas tradition in England. It's a tube, nicely wrapped with a small explosive inside so when you open it there's a loud pop. Inside is a token prize, a joke and a paper crown. Usually done at Christmas Dinner.

Chinless Wonder - *adj* - A person of upper class extraction who's clueless or lacks depth of character.

Chuff - *v* - Fart.

Chuffed - *adj* - To be quite pleased about something, not to be confused with the singular version above.

Chugger - *n* - Short for charity mugger, someone who prowls Britain's high streets and pressures people to donate money to charities (they earn a commission on each donation).

Chunder - *v* - To vomit.

Chunky Chips - n - Very thick cut French fries.

Cider - *n* - Alcoholic form of apple juice.

Ciggy - *n* - A cigarette.

Clear out – *v* – To have a good cleaning out of something.

Cling Film – *n* – Saran Wrap/plastic wrap

Clone town - *n* - The process where all the high streets in Britain have the same big chain stores so they all look pretty much the same and push out small local businesses.

Close - *n* - A cul-de-sac.

Clunge - *n* - A very very rude word for the female vagina not to be used in polite or even impolite conversation.

Coach - *n* - A bus.

Cobblers - *n* - Stupid nonsense. Similar to rubbish.

Cock - *adj* - A very versatile insult but basically an idiot.

Cock-up - *v* - To mess something up really badly.

Codswallop - *n* - Nonsense.

Colleague - *n* - Co-worker

College - *n* - A school that specializes in single year studies. Done between leaving school and going to a university.

Collywobbles - *n* - The heebie-jeebies.

Come a Cropper - *v* - To fail miserably.

Compensation – *n* – Damages or award for a court case.

Compulsory Purchase – *v* – An eminent domain seizure/sale.

Concession - *n* - A discount for a specific group (seniors, students, etc).

Confuddled - *v* - To be confused or not understand a situation.

Cooker - *n* - Otherwise known as an oven.

Cop off - *v* - Kiss.

Copper - *n* - Policeman.

Cor - *interj* - Ohhh!

Cor blimey - *interj* - Said to be an abbreviation of 'God Blind Me'. An interjection that has changed meaning over time. In early novels it was used in the same way as 'damn' to express exasperation or frustration. In recent years it is regarded as a mild expression of surprise or shock. Sometimes used to comic effect ('Blimey! It's the Rozzers!' - 'Goodness me! The police!'), in a deliberate reference to it being archaic usage.

Coriander - *n* - The herb cilantro.

Corn – *n* – Many grains are called Corn not just corn on the cob as we know it.

Corrie - *n* - Short for Coronation Street - a soap opera aired on ITV.

Costermonger – *n* – Fruit and vegetable pushcart vendor.

Cot - *n* - Baby crib.

Cot death - *n* - SIDS.

Cotton buds - *n* - Cotton swabs.

Cotton wool - *n* - Cotton ball.

Council house - *n* - Public housing or a housing project.

Courgette - *n* - Zucchini.

Court shoes - *n* - Woman's high heeled shoe - a pump.

Cow - adj - A woman of contempt - a rude bitch.

Cowboy - n - A dishonest or incompetent trade worker.

Cream Crackered - *adj* – Rhyming slang; to be extremely tired.

Creche - *n* - Day-care or nursery.

Crikey - *interj* - General expression of surprise.

Crisps - *n* - Potato Chips.

Croft – *n* – Small landholding.

Crossroads – *n* – A name for a 4-way American style intersection.

Crumbs - *interj* - A common expression of disappointment.

Crumpet - *n* - A yummy teacake.

Crusty Dragon - *n* - A booger.

Cupboard – *n* – A closet.

Cuppa - *n* - A cup of tea.

Current account - *n* - A checking account.

Curtains – *v* – To close or go out of business.

Cutlery - *n* - Silverware.

CV - *n* - Short for Curriculum Vitae but Americans would simply call it a Résumé.

D

Dab hand - *n* - To be particularly skilled at something.

Dabs - *n* - Fingerprints.

Daddy long-legs - *n* - Not to be confused with the type of spider, it actually refers to the crane fly.

Dado - *n* - A chair railing on a wall.

Daft - *adj* - An idiot, stupid, or foolish person. Can also refer to a thing or action that doesn't make sense or is ridiculous.

Daft Cow - *adj* - A rude and stupid overweight woman.

Dago - *n* - Derogatory term for a Spanish, Italian or foreign person.

Damp - *n* - Mold or wet rot that is common in older homes.

Damp Squib - *adj* - An event which you think will be exciting but which actually turns out to be a disappointment.

Damper - *n* - The shock absorber on a car.

Dangly-bits - *n* - Male genitalia.

Dapper - *adj* - A well dressed and well spoken individual, can be used as a compliment or an insult.

Daylight robbery - *n* - A highway robbery.

Dear - *adj* - Something that is expensive or costly.

Dekko --n - A look, glance - to take a look at something.

Demob – *n* - Discharged, to be discharged from military service.

De-mister - *n* - De-froster.

Destroyed - *adj* - To be very drunk or intoxicated on drugs.

Detached House – *n* – A free standing house.

Diamond Geezer - *n* - A respected older gentleman, phrase mainly used in London.

Diary - *n* - A person's schedule or calendar. Not a personal journal.

Dibbles - *n* - Police officer as in Officer Dibble from Top Cat.

Diddle - *v* - To swindle or con someone.

Digestive - *n* - A biscuit that you dunk in your tea, sort of like a cookie that's supposed to aid in digestion.

Dim - *adj* - Someone who is stupid.

Div - *adj* - An idiot.

Divvy - *n* - An idiot.

DIY - *abbr* - Shorthand for Do it Yourself - i.e. for home improvement projects. "Fancy doing a little DIY this weekend?"

Do - *n* - A party.

Doddle - *n* - Something that is very easy.

Dodgems - *n* - Bumper cars.

Dodgy - *adj* - Something shady or rather dubious. Also can apply to something that was poorly made or doesn't work well.

Dog-end - *n* - A cigarette butt.

Dogging - *v* - The act of having sex in public parks while people watch.

Dog's bollocks - *n* - Something especially good is "the dog's bollocks".

Dog's breakfast - *n* - A complete mess.

Dog's Dinner - *n* - The same meaning as 'dog's breakfast'.

Dogsbody - *n* - A lowly servant or functionary

Dole - *n* - The various forms of welfare are lumped under this term. To be on the Dole is to live off the state.

Done Over - *v* - To be beaten up by someone.

Donkey Work – *n* - The boring or laborious part of a job; drudgery.

Donkey's years - *n* - Something that happened a long time ago.

Dosh - *n* - Money.

Doss - *v* - To be lazy and not do much.

Doss House – *n* – Flophouse.

Double-barreled - *adj* - The practice of upper-class people having more than one last name joined together with a hyphen.

Dozy - *adj* - A person who is rather slow.

Draught - *n* - We say 'draft' as in a cold draft.

Draughts - *n* - The game of checkers.

Drawing-pin - *n* - A thumb tack.

Dressing gown - *n* - A bathrobe.

Drop Trou – *v* – To get naked or flash someone.

Drover – *n* - a person who moves groups of animals (such as cattle or sheep) from one place to another.

Dual carriageway - *n* - A divided highway a step down from a motorway.

Duff - *n* - Something that doesn't work.

Dummy - *n* - A baby's pacifier.

Dustbin - *n* - Garbage can.

Dustman - *n* - Garbage man.

Duvet - *n* - Bed cover.

Dux - *n* - The valedictorian at a school.

Dynamo - *n* - An electric generator.

E

Early Days – *inf* – Too soon; jumping the gun.

Earner - *n* - A job that earns good money.

Easy Peasy - *n* - Something that is really easy to do.

Eating irons - *n* - Silverware/cutlery

Ecosse - *n* - The French name for Scotland.

Eejit - *n* - An idiot.

Effing - *adj* - A polite way to say 'f*cking.'

Egg Banjo - *n* - A fried egg sandwich.

Elastoplast - *n* - A band-aid.

Electrics - *n* - The electrical fittings in a house.

Elevenses - *n* - Means having a snack mid-morning.

End-piece - *n* - End of the male genitalia - another way of saying "bell-end."

Engaged - *adj* - To be busy with something.

Enplane - *v* - To get onto an airplane.

Entail - *n* - An old English custom that controlled how a large estate was inherited and what could be done with it.

Entrée - *n* - The appetizer portion of a meal.

Essex girl - *adj* - Derogatory term for a girl from Essex that does not have any class.

Estate agent - *n* - A realtor or real estate agent and generally they're not very respected.

Estate car - *n* - A station wagon.

Eurosceptic - *n* - A person who is against British involvement in the European Union.

Eurocrat - *n* - A derogatory term for the civil servants that work at the center of the European Union.

Excluded – *v* – To be expelled from school.

Exercise Book – *n* – Notebook.

Ex-Council - *n* - An apartment or house that used to be public housing but has since been bought by the tenants (and perhaps sold on but it will always be known as ex-council).

Expat - *n* - Someone who lives abroad.

Eyetie - *n* - Someone from Italy - an offensive term.

F

Fab – *n* – Cool – short for fabulous.

Faff - *v* - To dither or screw around, pussyfoot around.

Fag - *n* - A cigarette.

Fag-end - *adj* - The used stub of a cigarette, and by extension the unpleasant and worthless loose end of any situation. "It was the Fag End of my shift, and I was knackered".

Faggot - *n* - A spiced meatball.

Fairy cake - *n* - Also known to Americans as a cupcake.

Fairy lights - *n* - The general name for Christmas Lights.

Fancy - *v* - To desire or want to do something. Often used lightheartedly to describe the act of being attracted to someone.

Fancy dress - *n* - To wear a costume often inspired by characters or individuals from popular culture.

Fancy dress party - *n* - A party where costumes are worn.

Fancy Man – *n* – A woman's lover.

Fanny - *n* - A woman's vagina. Not for use in polite conversation. Also used as an insult.

Father Christmas – *n* – Santa Claus.

Feck - *n* - An exclamation of anger of frustration similar to f*ck. Commonly attributed to Irish English.

Feeder – *n* – Child's Bib.

Fellow – *n* – Member of a college governing body.

Fête – *n* – Village or town fair.

Fiddle – *n* – To swindle someone. Living on the fiddle.

Fiddly Bits – *adj* –
Something petty or small
that is difficult to
manage.

Filch - *v* - To steal
something.

Flash - adj - Something
that is showy or
ostentatious.

Fillet Steak – *n* –
Tenderloin steak or Filet
Mignon.

Film - *n* - A movie. Brits
would generally say they
want to see a film not a
movie.

Filth - *n* - A not so nice
term for the police.

Fire Brigade – *n* - The
local fire department.

First Floor – *n* – What we
would call the second
floor in a building. The
ground floor is the first
level.

Fish fingers – *n* – Fish
Sticks.

Fishmonger – *n* – A store
where you buy fish. The
term also refers to the
person selling the fish.

Fit - *adj* – 1. A word used
to describe an attractive
woman or male. 2.
Seizures – to have a fit.

Fit for Purpose – *adj* –
Something doing what it
is designed to do – if
something is not fit for
purpose, it doesn't work.

Fitted - *v* - To have
something installed.

Fitter – *n* – Plumber or
mechanic who fixes or
installs something.

Fittings – *n* – Fixtures –
shop fixtures.

Fiver - *n* - Five pounds
sterling.

Fizzy drink - *n* - Soda-
pop or soft drink.

Flag - *adj* - To become
tired or lose all energy.

Flannel – *n* – Washcloth
or facecloth.

Flat - *n* - An apartment.

Flatmate - *n* - A
roommate in your flat.

Flat out – *inf* – At full
speed.

Flipping – *adj* – Darn.
"Flipping heck."

Flog - *n* - An attempt to
sell something that may
not be worth the money
being asked.

Fluff - *n* - Dryer lint.

Flutter - *v* - A brief go at
gambling.

Fly tipping - *v* - The act of dumping your trash in a place you're not supposed to.

Folly – *n* – Whimsical, pointless structure usually on a great estate.

Football - *n* - What Americans quaintly call soccer.

Football Pitch - *n* - A field where British Football is played.

Footie - *n* - A shorthand term for Football.

Footpath - *n* - A public path through the countryside for walking.

Forecourt – *n* – Front yard usually referred to a gas station pumping area.

Fortnight - *n* - Two weeks. Often used in the UK when talking about time.

Freehold - *n* - Owning both the land and the building on the land. Sometimes in Britain a different person owns the land and the building. See 'leasehold'.

Freehouse – *n* - A pub not affiliated with a specific brewery and can serve whatever beers it likes.

Freesat - *n* - A selection of free channels you can receive via satellite with a dish and a receiver.

Freeview - *n* - A selection of digital channels you can view for free if you purchase a Freeview receiver, which usually has added features.

Free Phone – *n* – A toll free phone number – what we would call a 1-800 number.

Fresher – *n* – Freshman – first year student at university.

Fringe - *n* - Hair bangs.

Frock – *n* – A dress.

Fry-up - *n* - Another name for the full English breakfast as most of the meal is fried in some form.

Full English - *n* - A full English breakfast usually consists of eggs, sausage, black pudding, bacon, mushrooms, baked beans, hash browns, and half a tomato.

Full Monty - *n* - The entire take or everything that is desired.

Full stop - *n* - Period. The type at the end of a sentence.

Fun fair - *n* - Carnival or amusement rides.

G

Gaffe - *n* - A home.

Gaffer - *n* - The boss.

Gaffer tape - *n* - Duct tape.

Gagging - *v* - Desperate in a derogatory way. i.e. She was gagging for it.

Garden - *n* - Back yard.

Gardening Leave – *n* - When a person gives notice for their job and they're sent home and told not to work during the notice period, but still get paid.

Gammon – *n* – Ham.

Garden – *n* – Yard.

Gash - *n* - Derogatory term used for the female genitalia.

Gatropub - *n* - A pub that serves food, sometimes pretentiously.

Gay - *adj* - Something that is bad, e.g. "It was 'gay' being mugged."

Gazump - *n* - To accept a higher offer on something at the last minute.

GCSE's - *n* - Academic tests that take place before the A-levels (many students stop here and 'graduate').

Gear lever - *n* - The stick shift in a manual car.

Gearbox - *n* - A car's transmission.

Geezer - *n* - Someone you respect.

Geordie - *n* - Someone from the Newcastle area. Made famous in Geordie Shore, a spin-off of MTV's Jersey Shore.

General Election – n – A countrywide election when MP's and the government are voted on.

Gentry – *n* – The landed class – people who own land or once did. The Aristrocracy.

Gen up – *n* – To fill in or bone up.

Geordle – *n* – A native of the Tyneside area of Northern England.

Get Knotted – *n* – Stop bugging me!

Get off - *v* - To make out with someone.

Get on - *v* - To do something. Commonly used in 'How did you get on?'

Get the Nod - *v* - To get permission to do something.

Get stuck in – *n* – To get involved deeply into something.

Get your end away - *v* - To have sex.

Gib – *n* – A person who lives in Gibraltar.

Giddy - *n* - To get dizzy or experience vertigo.

Ginger - *n* - A person with red hair.

Ginger beer - *adj* - Derogatory term for a homosexual.

Girl guide – *n* – Girl Scout.

Git - *n* - An incompetent, stupid, annoying, or childish person.

Give over - *interj* - To give up.

Give way - *interj* - To yield when driving.

Give You a Bell - *v* - Means to call someone on the phone.

Glasshouse – *n* – Greenhouse

Glaswegian – *n* – A native of Glasgow, Scotland.

Glop - *n* - Thick substance or unappetizing food.

G.M.T. – *abbrv* – Greenwich Mean Time.

Go - *v* - To try something. i.e. To give it a go.

Gob - *n* - Your mouth in a derogatory sense. Shot your gob!

Gobshite - *n* - Bullshit.

Gobsmacked - *adj* - Flabbergasted, dumbfounded, astounded, speechless.

Golf buggy - *n* - Golf cart.

Googly - *n* - A cricket ball that bounces around randomly when it lands.

Gone off - *v* - Something that's gone bad or expired.

Gormless - *adj* - Someone lacking in common sense.

Goss – *n* – Short for gossip. A goss mag is a celebrity gossip rag.

Grace and Favour – *n* - To be given a house/home by the government as part of your ministerial post (i.e. 10 Downing Street, etc).

Grammar - *n* - A textbook.

Grammar School - *n* - Elementary school.

Grand - *n* - Used in place of thousand (i.e. "This house is worth 140 grand").

Grasp the nettle – *inf* – Take the bull by the horns.

Grass - *n* - A snitch.

Great War – *n* – How Britons usually refer to the First World War. World War II is usually referred to as 'The War.'

Green fingers - *n* - Someone who is adept at the gardening arts.

Greenbelt - *n* - The land around cities and towns in Britain that is left undeveloped to preserve the environment.

Greenfield - *n* - Land that can't be developed or built upon that's left to exist for the purpose of pretty landscapes.

Gretna Green – *n* – Town on the Scottish border where couples could get a quick marriage Las Vegas style. To go 'Gretna Green' is to allope.

GP - *n* - General Practitioner - your regular family doctor.

Grizzle - *n* - To grumble or moan, see whingeing. Also a fussy baby.

Grit – *n* – Put down on roads in the winter to improve road conditions. It's not salt usually, but sand or gravel. A gritting truck drops the grit.

Grockle - *adj* - A derogatory term for a Tourist, primarily used in Southern England.

Grotty - *adj* - Something that is gross or cruddy.

Ground floor – n – First floor in a building.

Growler - *n* - A very rude term for female genitals covered in pubic hair.

Guff - *v* - Fart.

Guildhall – n – A town or city hall; center of government.

Guinea - *n* - A older unit of currency that meant 1 Pound and 1 Shilling. (see appendix).

Gutted - *adj* - To be devastated or shocked about something.

Guv'nor - *n* - The boss.

Gyp - *n* - Something that's an irritating pain.

H

Hacked-off - *adj* - Annoyed or stressed.

Haggis - *n* - Legendary Scottish dish consisting of a sheep's minced heart, liver, and lungs cooked in its own stomach with onion, oatmeal, and spices.

Haha - *n* - Trench dug at the end of a garden in place of a fence to the view isn't spoiled.

Hairdresser – *n* – A barber shop or beauty parlor.

Half past –n – 30 minute mark in an hour. Half hour.

Half term – *n* – Brief school vacation in the middle of a British school term.

Hand-luggage - *n* - Carry-on baggage.

Handbag - *n* - A woman's purse.

Handbags - *n* - A harmless fight

Handbrake - *n* - Parking/Emergency brake in a car.

Hansard – *n* – The official record of the Houses of Parliament.

Hard Done By – *n phrase* – To be harshly or unfairly treated.

Hard shoulder - *n* - Shoulder on the side of the road that's paved.

Harley St – *n* – Street in London where private Doctors practice – usually expensive and exclusive, not part of the NHS.

Harrovian – *n* – Someone who went to the exclusive public school Harrow (a private school in Britain is called a public school).

Hash - *n* - The # symbol.

Haulage Company – *n* – A trucking company.

Hawking – *v* – Door to door selling.

Have a go - *v* - To give something a try. Can also mean to have a fight.

Have a go hero - *n* - A person that attempts to defend their home or property against an intruder with force.

Haver - *n* - To ramble incoherently.

Having kittens - *interj* - To be extremely nervous.

Hay fever – *n* - The term generally used when talking about seasonal allergies.

Head – *n* – The Headmaster or Headmistress of a school. The American equivalent is the principal or dean.

Head boy - *n* - Highest achieving boy in a class similar to valedictorian.

Head girl - *n* - Highest achieving girl in a class similar to valedictorian.

Health and Safety - *n* - An all encompassing term of derision geared towards useless safety rules and regulations.

Heath – *n* – Wide open land, often wild and inaccessible.

Hedgerow – *n* – Living walls that line many fields and roads in Britain.

Helmet - *n* - 1. The glans of the penis 2. A fool.

Helter-skelter – *n* – A carnival/fun fair slide.

Hen night - *n* - Bachelorette party.

Her Majesty's pleasure - *v* - To be put into prison.

Higgledy-piggledy - *adj* - Something all jumbled up or in disarray.

High street - *n* - Main street.

High tea - *n* - Late afternoon light meal that usually involves a cup of tea.

Hill-walking - *n* – Hiking.

Hire - *v* - To rent something. i.e. A hire car.

Hire car - *n* - A rental car.

Hire purchase – *n* – To buy something on an installment plan.

Hoarding – *n* – A roadside billboard or sign.

Hob - *n* - A range or stove.

Hockey - *n* - Field hockey.

Holiday - *n* - What we would call a vacation or any time off of work. Brits usually get 28 days paid holiday. That's not a typo.

Home Office – *n* – Government department responsible for law enforcement and immigration.

Hoodie - *n* - A young person usually known for their misdeeds who are identified by their distinctive clothing, a hooded sweatshirt.

Hoover - *n* - A vacuum cleaner, regardless of brand.

Hoovering - *v* - The act of vacuuming.

Horses for Courses - *v* - To each his own.

Honours – *n* – Titles bestowed by the Queen for recognizing service to the British people. The most famous honour is a Knighthood allowing the person to be called Sir or Dame. There are many other types of honours. See appendix.

Hooligan – *n* – A hoodlum often associated with English football.

Housing Estate - *n* - A sub-division but it can also mean a public housing estate as well.

Hovis – n – Most famous British bread brand.

Hum - *n* - A bad smell.

Hundreds and thousands – *n* – Multicolored sprinkles, often put on cookies.

I

Icing sugar - *n* - Powdered sugar.

Ickle - *n* - Something very small.

In Care – *n* – In a foster home.

Industrial Action – *n* – Euphemism for strike.

Indicator - *n* - Turning signal in a car.

Innit - *interj* - Shortened from "ain't it" or isn't it.

Interval - *n* - Intermission or a break in performance.

Ironmonger - *n* - The old name for a hardware store. Can also be used to refer to the dealer of said hardware.

Ivories - *n* - Teeth.

J

Jabs - *n* - Vaccinations or shots.

Jacket potato - *n* - A baked potato.

Jam - *n* - Jelly.

Jam sandwich - *n* - A term for Police Car.

Jammy - *adj* - Someone who is lucky.

Jammy dodger - *n* - A lucky person. Also the name of a British biscuit (see entry for *biscuit*)

Janeite – *n* – Jane Austen fan.

Jelly - *n* - What the British call Jell-O™, not to be confused with Jam, see above.

Jerry - *n* - Someone from Germany, derogatory.

Jersey – *n* – Pullover; sweater.

Jiggery-pokery – *n* – Deceitful behavior.

Jim-jams - *n* – Pajamas (note: the British spelling is "pyjamas.")

Jock - *n* - A Scottish person, usually male.

Job Centre – *n*- Where you go to sign up for unemployment and look for a job.

Jobsworth - *n* - An official who strictly adheres to rules and regulations. See Health and Safety.

John Thomas - *n* - Male genitalia.

Joiner – *n* - Carpenter

Joint - *n* - A large piece of meat like a beef loin.

Jolly - *adv* - Very good.

Jollies - *n* - Pleasure or thrills.

Jubblies - *n* - A woman's breasts.

Jumble sale - *n* - A garage sale.

Jumped up - *adj* - Arrogant.

Jump leads - *n* - Car jumper cables.

Jumper - *n* - A sweater.

K

Kagoul - *n* - A poncho or windbreaker jacket.

KBO – *abbrv* – Keep Buggering On. Churchill's favorite catchphrase meaning to get going no matter the challenge.

KC – *abbr* - King's Counsel during the reign of a **king**, is an eminent **lawyer** (usually a **barrister**) who is appointed by the **Queen** to be one of "Her Majesty's Counsel learned in the law."

Kecks - *n* - Pants or trousers.

Keen on – *inf* – To be enthusiastic. He was keen on her.

Keep – *v* – To raise something. He kept pigs in his back garden.

Kerb - *n* - A curb.

Kerb crawler - *n* - A person who solicits street prostitutes.

Kerfuffle - *n* - To make a big fuss about something.

Kip - *n* - A word for sleep or to get some sleep (have a kip).

Kipper – *n* – A young child or toddler.

Kirby grip - *n* - Bobby pin.

Kissing gate – n – A cattle gate where only people can pass through, sometimes romantically.

Kit - *n* - Clothing or sports equipment.

Kitchen roll - *n* - Paper towel.

Kiwi - *n* - Someone from New Zealand.

Knackered - *adj* - Exhausted, tired, also 'broken'

Knackers - *n* - Vulgar name for testicles.

Knees-up - *n* - A party.

Knickers - *n* - Women's underwear, see pants.

Knob - *n* - Male genitalia.

Knobhead - *adj* - A stupid, irritating person.

Knob jockey - *adj* - Homosexual, derogatory.

Knob-end - *adj* - An idiot, or tip of penis (see bell-end).

Knock about - *n* - Sporting practice.

Knock up - *v* - To bang on someone's door. Does not mean to impregnate.

Know your onions - *phrs* - To be very knowledgeable on a particular subject.

L

L-plates - *n* - Special license plates you're required to have on your car while learning to drive in the UK.

Lad - *n* - A boy or an immature grown male.

Lad mag – *n* - A men's magazine that usually features nudity or near nudity.

Laddette - *n* - An immature woman.

Ladybird - *n* - A ladybug.

Lager - *n* - A type of beer popular in England.

Lager lout - *n* - A person who misbehaves while drunk.

Lairy - *adj* - To be noisy or abusive.

Landslip – *v* - Landslide

Larder - *n* - Pantry.

Lav - *n* - Short for lavatory.

Lay-by - *n* - Rest area along the highways.

Lead – *n* – Leash, like for a dog.

Leet – *adj* – mad, crazy, insane.

Leasehold - *n* - A possessory right to live in a building or flat but not owning the land upon which it sits. Common for apartments. Leases are usually for 99 or 999 years.

Leaver – *n* – A graduating student. School leaver.

Leccy – *n* – Electricity.

Left luggage - *n* - A place you can leave your luggage safely (for a fee) while you travel or shop.

Leg it - *v* - To run hurriedly.

Leg over - *n* - Sexual intercourse.

Lemonade - *n* - While in the UK if you ask for Sprite or 7-up you'll be given this which is basically carbonated lemonade.

Letter-box – *n* – Mailbox.

Level crossing – *n* – Railway crossing level with the ground.

Licenced – *adj* – Possessing a liquor license to sell alcohol.

Lido – *n* – Public open air swimming pool.

Lie-in - *n* - The act of sleeping in.

Life Peer – *n* – A title or honor given to you that only exists for the rest of your life – not hereditary. Entitles you to sit in the House of Lords.

Lift - *n* - An elevator.

Limey - *n* - An English person. Derogatory Americanism.

Lino – *n* – Shortened version of Linoleum.

Livery – *n* – Costume or uniform. Example – what a servant would wear in a great house serving dinner.

Local - *n* - The local pub.

Lodger - *n* - A person who rents a room in your home, lower on the scale than a flatmate.

Loft - *n* - The attic area of a house.

Lolly - *n* - A popsicle.

Long-stay – *adj* – Long-term. For example – the long stay car park.

Loo - *n* - The bathroom. Also used to describe the physical toilet.

Lorry - *adj* - A semi or heavy goods truck.

Lost Property Office – *n* – Lost and found.

Lost the Plot - *n* - Someone who's gone mad.

Lounge – *n* – The living room in a house.

Love - *n* - A kind form of address ("Excuse me, love").

Luv - *n* - Honey or darling.

M

M&S - *abbr* - Shorthand for the department store Marks and Spencer, the British equivalent to JC Penney. Also affectionately known as Marks and Sparks.

Macintosh - *n* - Light waterproof jacket, also known as a Mac.

Mad - *adj* - Crazy.

Made Redundant - *v* – To be laid off you're your job, someone whose job no longer exists.

Magistrate – *n* – Justice of the peace.

Maisonette - *n* - A set of rooms for living in, typically on two stories of a larger building and with its own entrance from outside.

Maize – *n* – Corn.

Managing Director – n – The chief executive of a company or chairman. Usually the top most person in charge.

Manc - *n* - Someone from Manchester.

Mancunian - *n* - A polite way to say someone is from Manchester.

Manifesto – *n* – Document put out by a political party during an election that lays out its promises of what they'll do if they win. Usually considered a binding document.

Manky - *adj* - Dirty or filthy.

Manual gearbox - *n* - A manual transmission on a car.

Marmite - *n* - A strange spread usually eaten on toast made of yeast extract. An acquired taste often listed as one of the tops things Brits living abroad miss from home.

Marquee – *n* - An outside tent - like you'd set up for a wedding.

Marrow - *n* - The vegetable squash.

Mash – *n* – Mashed potatoes.

Mashed - *n* - High from smoking cannabis.

Mate - *n* - A good friend.

Mates Rates – *n* – Getting your friends to do something for you for a discount or for free or get paid in lager.

Maths - *n* - Mathematics. They say the S.

Meat and two veg - *n* - Male external genitalia.

Mend – *v* – To fix something or have something repaired.

Mere – *n* – Lake.

Mental - *n* - Crazy or insane.

Mews - *n* - The short narrow street behind a house like an alleyway.

Mews house - *n* - Small house located on a mews street that often housed servants and horses but have since been converted into homes.

Miffed - *adj* - Pissed off.

Mileometer - *n* - A car's odometer.

Mince - *n* - Ground beef.

Mince pie - *n* - A sweet pie usually enjoyed at Christmas stuff with fruit and mincemeat (which is not actually meat).

Mind - *v* - To be aware of. "Mind the Gap."

Minge - *n* - Female genitalia, derogatory.

Minger - *adj* - An ugly or filthy-minded person. There is usually an implication of poor hygiene or body odor in the usage.

Minted - *n* - To be wealthy.

Mobile phone - *n* - We would say cell phone or cellular phone. Most Brits just say mobile.

Moggy - *n* - A cat.

Mole grip - *n* - Vise grip.

Molly-coddled - *adj* - To be overly looked after.

Mong - *n* - Derogatory term for someone with special needs.

Monged (out) - *n* - To be severely drunk or high.

Moose - *n* - A very unattractive woman

Moreish - *adj* - To want more of something.

Moses Basket – *n* – A baby's bassinet.

Most Secret – *adj* – Top Secret.

Mothering Sunday – *n* – Mother's Day, usually the 4th Sunday during Lent.

Motor - *n* - An antiquated term for an automobile.

Motorway - *n* - The equivalent would be an interstate highway.

Move house - *v* - To move to a new house.

Multi-story car park - *n* - A parking garage.

Muck in - *v* - To help with or assist in something.

Muggins - n - A simple person or someone silly.

Mum - *n* - Mother.

Munter - *n* - An ugly person.

Muppet - *n* - An idiot.

N

Naff - *adj* - Something that tacky or otherwise in poor taste.

Nail Bar – *n* – Nail salon.

Nail varnish – *n* – Nail polish.

Nappy - *n* - Baby's diaper

Narked - *adj* - Being in a bad mood

National Insurance – *n* – Government mandated insurance system, equivalent would be Social Security in the USA.

Natter - *n* - Chatter.

Natty - *adj* - Cool.

Naturist – *n* - Nudist

Naughty bits - *n* - A polite way to say male genitalia.

Nause - *adj* - An annoying person.

Navvy - *n* - Road or construction worker.

Nearside - *n* - The side of the car that's closest to the curb.

Nervy – *v* – To be nervous or jumpy.

Newsagent - *n* - A convenience store where you can buy newspapers, magazines and snacks and drinks. Also known as a newsy.

Newsreader – n – News presenter on TV or radio.

NHS – *abbr* – National Health Service. Britain's nationalized health system.

Nick - *v* - To steal or arrest.

Nicked - *v* - To be arrested or something that was stolen.

Niggle - *v* - To pester.

Nil – *n* – Nothing, zero.

Nimrod - *adj* - Another name for a weasel, but also used to called someone stupid.

999 – *n* – Emergency services phone number. The British equivalent of 911.

Nip - *v* - To go off and do something quickly.

Nippy - *adj* - Cold.

Nip round – *inf* – To pop over or come around to someone's house.

Nob - *n* - A member of the nobility class.

Nonce - *n* - A pedophile.

Non-conformist – *n* – A person who does not follow the Church of England.

Non-starter - *n* - An idea so absurd it has no chance of being a success.

Nosey parker - *n* - A person who gossips and won't mind their own business.

Nosh - *n* - Food.

Notice board – *n* – Bulletin board.

Nought - *n* - The number zero.

Noughts and crosses - *n* - The game of tic-tac-toe.

Nowt - *n* - Nothing.

Number plate - *n* - License plate.

Numpty - *n* - An idiot.

Nutter - *n* - A crazy person.

O

O-levels - *n* - Series of exams that took place a few years before you're A-levels. Replaced by the GCSEs in the 1980's.

OAP - *Acronym* - Old Age Pensioner - someone living on social security.

Off one's onion - *adj* - Crazy.

Off one's rocker - *adj* - Crazy.

Off one's tits - *adj* - High on drink or drugs.

Off one's trolley - *adj* - Crazy.

Off-license - *n* - An off license is a place where you can buy alcohol and other small household goods. I.e. the corner shop. Also known as the offie.

Offside - *n* - 1. The side of the car that is farthest from the curb. 2. Complicated rule in football that generates endless debate.

Oi - *interj* - Hey!

Old Bill - *n* - The police.

Old banger - *n* - An old crappy car.

OH - *n* - Other half - significant other.

Omnibus - *n* - 1. A gathering of a week's radio shows or a soap opera into one large episode. 2. What they used to call buses.

Omnishambles – *n* – A situation that is messed up in multiple ways. Coined by Malcolm Tucker in *The Thick of It*.

On offer – *n* – To be 'on sale' in a retail setting.

On the blink - *adj* - Something that doesn't work.

On the fiddle - *phrs* - Cheating.

On the piss - *v* - getting drunk, drinking alcohol.

On the pull - *v* - Out looking for sex.

One - *n* - Referring to yourself in the third person, The Royal We.

One Off - *n* - A special or one time event.

Open Day – *n* – Open House, usually for prospective students to gain insight into a college or university

Orbital – *n* – Another name for a ringroad.

Outgoings – **n** – Business or personal expenses.

Overdraft – *n* – Bank loan linked to your checking account.

Overtake – *v* – To pass on the road.

Oxbridge – *n, adj* – A portmeanteau of Oxford and Cambridge used to refer to a person who attended either or a particular 'Oxbridge' mindset. The ivory tower. Used to separate the two oldest universities from other 'lesser' provincial universities.

P

P45 - *n* - The form used when someone is being fired or made redundant.

P.A. - *n* - A personal assistant, secretary.

Page 3 – *n* - Page three of the daily newspaper The Sun used to feature a topless woman known as the Page 3 girl. The practice was discontinued in 2015.

Pack it in - *v* - To give up.

Pantomime - *n* - A strange tongue in cheek play often performed at Christmas time that's popular with families. A panto has to be seen to be understood.

Pants - *n* - 1. Someone's underwear. 2. Something that is total crap.

Paracetamol - *n* - The British equivalent to Tylenol.

Paraffin - *n* - Liquid kerosene.

Park and Ride – *n* - A parking lot located outside of a cramped city center than provides frequent bus access to said city center.

Parky - *adj* - Cold or chilly.

Partner – *n* – A gender neutral term for boyfriend/girlfriend.

Pastille - *n* - A type of small candy.

Pasty - *n* - A meat or vegetable filled pastry originating in Cornwall.

Patience - *n* - The card game of solitaire.

Pavement - *n* - The sidewalk.

Pear-shaped - *adj* - Something that's gone wrong.

Pebbledash – *n* – Pebble coated stucco – very common house covering.

Peckish - *adj* - To be a little hungry.

Peculiar - *adj* - Something that is unique.

Paedo - n - Shorthand phrase for pedophile (spelled *paedophile* in Britain).

Peeler – *n* – Bobby or Policeman.

Peer – *n* – A member of titled nobility – a Lord or Lady.

Pelican crossing - *n* - A type of crosswalk on British streets.

Penny dreadful – *n* – A cheap, low quality pulp novel.

Penny-farthing – *n* – An early two high wheeled bicycle.

Pensioner - *n* - An elderly person that's retired and collects their state pension.

People Carrier – *n* – A Mini-van.

Pergola – *n* – Trellis.

Perspex - *n* - Plexiglass..

Pet Hate – *adj* – Pet Peeve

Pervy - *adj* - Perverted.

Petrol - *n* - Gasoline.

Petrol bomb – *n* – Molotov cocktail.

Phone box *n* - Phone booth.

Phut - *adj* - Gone out, something that's stopped working.

Pig's ear - *n* - To make a mess out of something.

Pikey - *n* - A pejorative term used, mainly in England to refer to gypsies or people of low social class, offensive.

Pillar-box – *n* – Mailbox.

Pillock - *n* - An idiot.

Pimm's - *n* - A summery alcoholic drink popular in the UK.

Pinch - *v* - To steal.

Pint - *n* - A standard unit of drink measurement in the UK that's roughly equal to 20 ounces.

Pips - *n* - Seeds

Piss-artist - *n* - A frequent drunkard.

Pissed - *adj* - Drunk

Pissed up - *adj* - Drunk

Pitch - *n* - Grassy surface suitable for football or cricket.

Plane-spotter - *n* - A person who hangs around airports and looks at airplanes.

Planning Permission - *n* - The process of getting a building permit in the UK, often involving several layers of government and approvals. Can take years.

57

Plaster - *n* - A band-aid.

Plastered - *adj* - Extremely drunk

Plasticine - *n* - A type of modeling clay used to make Wallace and Gromit.

Plimsolls - *n* - Canvas shoes with a rubber sole.

Plod - *n* - The police

Plonker - *adj* - An idiot.

Plus One Channel – *n* – A channel where everything airs one hour later than the original channel to allow people to watch on a different schedule.

PMT – *abrv* - How British women refer to PMS - short acronym for Premenstrual tension.

Po-faced - *adj* – Glum or impassive.

Polo-neck - *n* - A turtleneck sweater.

Polling-day - *n* - Election day.

Polling place – *n* - Place where you vote.

Polytechnic – *n* – Community college, usually vocational.

Ponce - *n* - A homosexual, derogatory.

Pong - *n* - A bad smell.

Pongo - *n* - An infantryman in the military.

Pop round – *v* - Stop by for an informal chat as in "Later I will pop round for a visit."

Porkies - *n* - Lies.

Porridge – *n* – Cooked oatmeal.

Portakabin - *n* - Pre-fabricated building often used as a temporary office.

Portaloo - *n* - Portajohn.

Porter – *n* - Doorman.

Posh - *adj* - Someone or something that is very high class.

Post - *n, v* - 1. The mail. To post something is to mail something. 2. The post is also your daily delivery of mail.

Post Box – *n* – Mailbox.

Postal Vote – *n* – Absentee ballot.

Postcode – *n* – Zip code but more precise.

Post-free – *n* - Freepost or mail that is postage paid.

Postgraduate - *n* - A university level grad student.

Pot noodle - *n* - Ramen noodle soup.

Potholing - *n* - Spelunking.

Potplant - *n* - A potted plant.

Potty - *adj* - A little loopy or nuts.

Power Cut - *n* - An electricity black out.

Poxy - *adj* - Crappy.

Pram - *n* - Baby's stroller.

Prang - *n* - Minor car accident.

Prat - *n* - A particular type of idiot, jerk, or asshole.

Prawn - *n* - Shrimp.

Prefect - *n* - Head boy in a school.

Premium Bond – *n* – Government sponsored lottery savings bond.

Prep school - *n* - A type of boarding school for children.

Presenter - *n* - A radio or TV anchorperson.

Prezzy – *n* – A present or gift.

Proper – v – To have something done or do something properly. "He's done a proper job."

Pub - *n* - Public house, the local bar.

Pub Grub - *n* - Simple food usually served in pubs or bars. Fish and Chips is a great example of Pub Grub. Differs from the type of food served in a gastropub, which is fancier.

Public school - *n* - Despite the confusing name, a public school is actually a private exclusive school like Harrow or Eton. Also called an 'independent school'.

Pudding - *n* - The dessert part of meal - not actual pudding.

Pukka - *interj* - The genuine article.

Pull - *v* – To woo someone, usually in a club setting, with whom you might make out or have sex.

Pumps - *n* - Gym shoes.

Puncture - *n* - Flat tire.

Punt - *v* - To give something a try,

Punter - *n* - A customer or patron.

Purse - *n* - A little bag that holds change.

Pushchair - *n* - A child's stroller where the child sits upright.

Put paid - *v* - To settle a matter.

Pylon – *n* – High tension electrical wire tower.

Pyramid Selling – *v* – Pyramid Scheme – multi-level marketing scam.

Q

QC – *abbr* - A Queen's Counsel or King's Counsel during the reign of a **king**, is an eminent **lawyer** (usually a **barrister**) who is appointed by the **Queen** to be one of "Her Majesty's Counsel learned in the law."

Quango - *Acronym* - Quasi-autonomous non-governmental organization. An organization that's usually started by the government or has governmental powers that's not run by the government. It is usually a place to send troublesome politicians by giving them cushy jobs. Examples are the BBC and Visit Britain. See, TV show *Yes, Minister.*

Quay - *n* - A dock where boats are unloaded. Pronounced key.

Queue - *n, v,* - A line or to stand in line.

Quid - *n* - 1 Pound Sterling (e.g. "That car only costs 500 quid.")

Quids-in - *n* - To be in profit or to be all in on something.

Quim - *n* - Female genitalia.

Quite - *n* - A general term that means 'kind of'.

R

RADA – *Abbr* – Royal Academy of Dramatic Arts.
RAF – *abbr* – Royal Air Force.
Raid – *n* – Burglery
Rag & bone man - *n* - A scavenger who makes value out of garbage.
Randy - *adj* - To be sexually aroused.
Rates – *n* – Taxes – usually local business taxes.
Rat-arsed - *adj* - Quite drunk.
Razz - *v* - Vomit.
Read – *v* – To major in a subject at a university. 'He read history at Oxford.'
Reckon - *adv* - To believe something is true.
Recovery Services – *n* – Tow truck or roadside assistance.

Redundant – *adj* – To become unemployed. Phrase used when someone loses their job, their fired or their job no longer exists. "Phil was made redundant last week."
Refuse tip – *n* – Garbage dump.
Registration - *n* - A car's license plate (see also number plate).
Removers – *n* – Movers.
Removal men - *n* - A moving company that helps you move house.
Return ticket - *adj* - A round-trip ticket.
Rent boy - *n* - A male prostitute.
Revise - *v* - To study for exams.
Right - *adj* - To emphasize the meaning of something. "He was a right git."
Ring piece - *n* - The anus.
Rocket - *n* - Arugula salad.
Rodger - *v* - To have sex.
Romp - *v* - To have sex.

Ropey - *adj* - Something that's rather iffy.

Rot – *n* – Nonsense. "What rot!"

Roundabout - *n* - A traffic circle.

Row - *n, pron* - An argument.

Rozzer - *n* - A police officer.

RSPCA - *Acronym* - Royal Society for the Prevention of Cruelty to Animals.

Rubber - *n* - An eraser (does not mean a condom).

Rubbish - *n* - 1. Garbage 2. A nicer way to say bullshit. 3. To criticize.

Ruddy – *adj* - Damned

Rump steak – *n* – Sirloin steak.

Runner - *v* - To run out on the bill at a restaurant.

Rucksack - *n* - Backpack.

S

Sack - *v* - To fire someone or be fired from your job.

Saloon - *n* - Standard 4 door family sedan car.

Salt Beef – *n* – Corned Beef.

Samey - *adj* - Something that's similar.

Samaritans – *n* – An organization and phone hotline known for helping people thinking about suicide. If you need help, they have people standing by to help.

Sarnie - *n* - Sandwich.

Sassenach – *n* – A derogatory word for English used by the Scottish and Irish. From the Gaelic word for Saxon.

Satnav – *n* – GPS mapping device.

Savoury - *n* - Non-dessert food.

Scarper - *v* - To run away.

Scone - *n* - Buttery biscuit, usually served with tea with clotted cream and jam.

Scotch egg - *n* - A Scotch egg consists of a hard-boiled egg wrapped in sausage meat, coated in breadcrumbs and deep-fried.

Scouser - *n* - Someone from Liverpool.

Scheme – *n* – Plan. In America, this word has a negative connotation indicating a scam. In the UK it does not – it's a plan for something.

School-leaver – *n* – High-school graduate.

Scrotty - *adj* - Dirty.

Scrubber - *n* - Someone who is dirty or perceived poor, an offensive term. Derogatory term for "loose" woman also.

Scrummy - *adj* - Something that is delicious.

Scrumpy - *n* - Alcoholic apple cider.

Scullery – *n* – Back kitchen.

Scullery Maid – n – Kitchen maid can also do other dirty housework.

Scupper - *v* - To obstruct.

Sectioned - *v* - To be committed to a mental health facility against your will.

See a man about a dog - *v phrs* - Attend a secret deal or meeting or to go to the toilet.

Second(ment) – *v* – To transfer temporarily.

Sell-by-date - *n* - Expiration date (like on food).

Sellotape - *n* - Scotch tape.

Semi-detached - *n* - Usually a pair of houses that share a common wall and are mirror images of each other - a duplex. Also, called a 'semi' for short.

Send down – *v* – To be expelled from school.

Sent down - *v* - To be sent to prison.

Septic - *n* - An American. From Cockney Rhyming Slang, as in Septic Tank (rhymes with yank).

Serviette - *n* - Napkin.

Service Flat – *n* – Hotel style apartment.

Shag - *v* - To have sex.

Shambles - *adj* - A chaotic mess of something.

Shambolic - *adj* - Something in complete disarray similar to a shambles.

Shandy - *n* - A mixture of lager with Lemonade (see definition of lemonade.)

Shares – *n* – Stocks, like in a company.

Shat - *n* - Another way of saying 'shit' but in the past tense.

Shattered - *adj* - To be emotionally devastated or extremely tired.

Shedload - *n* - A large quantity of something.

Shilling - *n* - A form of currency before Britain switched to the decimal that means five pence.

Shingle – *n* – Beach pebbles. On a Shingle Beach.

Shirty - *adj* - Irritable.

Shite *n* - Shit.

Shop - *n* - A store.

Sick - *n* - The standard term for vomit or to throw up. "Oh man, I'm covered in sick."

Sickie - *n* - To take a day off of work or school but not actually be sick.

Side – *n* – Team.

Simple – *n* – Someone who is not very smart or not all there mentally.

Single – *n* – One-Way ticket.

Single-track – *n* - One lane road.

Sirloin – *n* – Porterhouse steak.

Sitting – *n* – Serving. "He was sitting on the library board."

Sixth Form – *n* – The final year of schooling for students who are university bound. A pupil in Sixth Form is called a Sixth Former.

Skinfull - *n* - The amount of alcohol needed to make one drunk.

Skint - *adj* - To be broke.

Skip - *n* - Dumpster.

Skipping - *v* - Dumpster diving.

Skirting board - *n* - Baseboard.

Skive - *v, n* - To be lazy or take an unwarranted day off, pull a sickie.

Skivvies - *n* - Another word for underwear or undergarments.

Slag - *v* - A whore. To call a woman a slag is a grievous insult.

Slag off - *v* - To denigrate someone, start rumors, usually in the victim's absence.

Slap - *n* - Cosmetic make-up, used in a derogatory way to indicate the person is wearing too much.

Slap head - *n* - A bald man.

Slapper - *n* - A slut.

Slash - *v* - To urinate.

Sledge – *n* – Sled.

Sleeper - *n* - Railroad tie.

Sleeping policemen - *n* - A speed bump in the road.

Sleep Rough – *v* – Sleeping in the open – usually referring to homeless people.

Slip-road – *n* - An exit on/off ramp on a highway.

Sloane Ranger – *n* – Derogatory term for the well off women who lived around Sloan Square. Fallen out of use.

Smarties - *n* - A chocolate candy similar to M&M's but are unrelated to the American candy also called Smarties.

Smashing - *adj* - Awesome!

Smeg - *n* - Smeg is a vulgarism or expletive used throughout the TV Show *Red Dwarf*. Although no specific meaning is ever given, it and its derivatives are regularly used as a derogatory term.

Snakes and ladders - *n* - The board game chutes and ladder.

Snap Election – *v* – Calling a surprise election before one is due.

Snog - *v* - Passionate kissing, not sex.

Snug – *n* – A room, often in a pub, that is more private.

Sod - *n, v, adj* - An idiot, moron, or annoying person. A bastard.

Sod's Law – *adj* - Sod's law is a name for the axiom that "if something can go wrong, it will", with the further addendum, in British culture, that it will happen at "the worst possible time". This may simply be construed, again in British culture, as "Expect the best, plan for the worst."

Sod Off - *v* - To tell someone to 'piss off.'

Soft-Shoulder - *n* - Roadside shoulder that's made of gravel.

Soldiers - *n* - Little strips of bread used for dipping into a boiled egg.

Solicitor - *n* - A lawyer that deals with contracts and other personal legal matters and can represent clients in lower courts, not a barrister.

Sorted - *adj* - A problem that has been fixed.

Sort out – *v* – Work out or take care of. Sorted (see above).

Sound - *adj* - To be reliable or trustworthy.

Soup, The – *n* – To be in trouble.

Spaghetti junction – n – Cloverleaf style interchange.

Spanner - *n* - A wrench. Commonly used in the phrase to 'throw a spanner in the works' meaning to break something.

Spare - *adj, n* - 1. To be at one's wits end. 2. Used in reference to the younger sibling of the heir to the throne (i.e. Prince Harry).

Spare room – *n* – Guest bedroom.

Spastic - *n* - A very insulting and derogatory term for someone who is mentally challenged.

Speedo - *n* - British abbreviation for the speedometer - not to be confused with the article of clothing.

Spend a penny – *v* – To go to the bathroom in a public restroom that requires payment. Modern usage broadly means to urinate in general.

Spiv - *n* – Smooth operator.

Spongle - *n* - Someone who is high on drugs.

Spotted dick - *n* - A type of spongecake with raisins in it.

Sport - *n* - The British say Sport as a plural instead of Sports.

Sports day – *n* – Annual track and field day.

Spot on - *adj* - Perfectly correct.

Spots - *n* - Pimples, zits.

Sprog - *n* - A young child.

Squiffy – *adj* - Something that's gone wrong. Also someone who is slightly drunk: tipsy.

Stabilisers - *n* - Training wheels on a bicycle.

Stag night - *n* - A bachelor party.

Stargazey Pie – *n* – A type of fish pie unique to Cornwall that usually has the heads sticking out.

Starkers - *v* - To be completely naked. A variant of this phrase is *stark bollock naked*.

Starter - *n* - The appetizer portion of a meal.

Steady on - *interj* - Hold your horses.

Steaming - *adj* - Extremely drunk, or extremely angry.

Sterling - *adj* - Awesome!

STI – *abbv* – Sexually transmitted infection; an STD. The British say STI instead.

Stick - *n* - Walking stick or cane.

Sticking plaster - *n* - A band-aid.

Sticky Wicket – *adj* – Originally a cricket term but now used to mean a difficult situation (without us attempting to explain Cricket).

Stockings - *n* - Ladies tights.

Stockist – *n* – Retailer.

Stodgy - *adj* - Something that's old fashioned.

Stone - *n* - A strange unit of measure unique to Britain and Ireland that measures 14 lbs usually used to measure the weight of a person.

Stonking - *adj* - Something really big.

Straight away - *interj* - Right away.

Strawberry Creams - *n* - A woman's breasts.

Streaky bacon – *n* – American style bacon.

Strimmer - *n* - A weed-whacker.

Stroppy - *adj* - Unreasonably grumpy.

Struck off – *v* – To be disbarred or lose a professional license.

Stuck in – *v* - To get wrapped up in a task or job.

Stuffed - *v* - Sexual intercourse (i.e. 'get stuffed'). Also, telling someone to *get stuffed* is akin to saying leave me alone, go away.

Subject – *n* – Citizen. Sort of. Britons are not citizens, they are subjects of the British crown.

Subway - *n* - A pedestrian walkway located underground.

Sultana - *n* - A golden/white raisin.

Sun cream - *n* - Sunscreen. Sometimes sun tan lotion.

Superannuation Scheme – *n* – Pension plan.

Surgery – *n* - 1. Doctor's or Dentist's office. 2. When an MP meets with his/her constituents.

Surveyor – *n* – Building inspector.

Suspenders - *n* - Garters.

Suss - *v* - To figure something out.

Swan Upping – *v* –
Annual ceremony where
all the Queen's swans
are counted on the
Thames (by right the
Queen owns all mute
swans in England).

Swede - *n* - Rutabega.

Sweets - *n* - Candy.

Sweet shop – *n* – Candy
store.

Swift half - *n* - A half pint
of beer or lager.

Swingeing – adj –
Whopping, huge. "The
government made
swingeing cuts."
Pronounced like
Whingeing.

Swimming costume - *n* -
Bathing suit.

Swizz - *n* - A small con.

Swot - *n* - To cram for a
test, to study hard.

T

Ta - *interj* - A simple thank you.

Tackle - *n* - Male genitalia.

Tad - *adj* - A little bit of something.

Tail-Back – *n* – Traffic back-up.

Take-away - *n, v* - 1. A fast food establishment. 2. The act of getting food and taking it home.

Take Into Care – *v* – When a child is removed from the parents and put into foster care.

Taking the mickey - *interj* - Pulling one's chain.

Taking the piss - *n* - Mocking, taking advantage of someone.

Tally-ho! - *interj* - Goodbye!

Tannoy - *n* – Brand name used to refer to all Public Address (PA) systems.

Tarmac - *n* - A paved road.

Tarrif – *n* – Schedule of charges like for a B&B stay or admissions charges.

Tart - *n* - Prostitute or loose woman.

Tart up – *v* – Doll up.

Tat - *n* - Cheap piece of junk, usually applied to souvenirs.

Ta-ta - *inter* – Bye-bye.

Tatty - *n* - A description for something that's tired and out of fashion. Like an old Seaside resort town.

Tea - *n* - Also known as tea-time, it's an evening meal.

Tea-break - *n* - Coffee break.

Tea-towel - *n* - A dish cloth.

Telepest – *n* – Telemarketer.

Telly - *n* - Short for television.

Tenner – *n* – Ten pound note.

Term – *n* – School year division – a trimester.

Terraced Houses - *n* - A series of conjoined houses that line a street and all look the same.

Tetchy - *adj* - Irritable.

Thankful Village – *n* – Also called Blessed Village are settlements in England that didn't lose anyone in World War I. A Doubly Thankful Village is one where no one was lost in either World War. There are 53 Thankful Villages in England and Wales.

The Times – *n* – National Newspaper of record, pillar of the British Establishment.

Throttle – *n* – Gas pedal in a car.

Thrupney bits - *n* - Woman's breasts.

Tick - *n* - To check something off on a list.

Ticket Tout – *n* – A ticket scalper.

Tickety-boo - *adj* - When something is going smoothly or proceeding quickly.

Tights - *n* - Pantyhose.

Till - *n* - Check-out counter in a store.

Tinpot – *n* – Crappy.

Tip - *n* - A garbage dump or a place that's a mess.

Tippex - *n* - Whiteout or liquid paper (something that's rarely used much anymore).

Tipple - *n* - A civilized alcoholic beverage.

Tire puncture – *n* – A flat tire.

Titchy - *n* - Something that is very small.

Tits up - *adj* - Something that's gone all wrong.

Todger - *n* - Male genitalia.

Toe-rag - *n* - A total scumbag.

Toff - *n* - Someone who is from the upper classes, it's slightly derogatory.

Tomato sauce - *n* - Ketchup/catsup.

Tommy – *n* – A private in the British army.

Top Gear – *n* – 1. Highest Gear. 2. Renowned motoring TV show.

Top-up - *v* - To top off something, make it full or add to it.

Torch - *n* - Flashlight.

Tory – *n* – Member of the Conservative Party.

Tosh - *adj* - Nonsense.

Tosser - *adj* - A person who likes to pleasure themselves but generally used as an insult against an arsehole.

Touch-up - *v* - To feel up or grope.

Tourist tat – *n* – Cheap souvenirs.

Traffic Light – *n* – Stop light.

Trailer tent - *n* - A pop-up camper.

Train-spotter - *n* - A person who stands around waiting for interesting trains.

Trainers - *n* - Gym shoes.

Tram - *n* - A streetcar - basically a bus on rails.

Tramp - *n* - Homeless person.

Travellers - *n* - A group of people who travel around Britain and live in makeshift campsites - often illegally, modern day Gypsies. Sometimes called Irish Travellers, but they're not always Irish. They're universally hated by everyone as they often cause a blight on the landscape.

Treacle - *n* - Molasses.

Trilby - *n* - A type of men's hat.

Trolley - *n* - A shopping cart in a store.

Trollop - *n* - A woman with loose morality.

Trolly dolly - *n* - Air stewardess, derogatory.

Trots, the - *n* - Diarrhea.

Trousers - *n* - Pants/slacks.

Trump – *n* – A fart, breaking wind.

Truncheon – *n* – Billy club.

Tube - *n* - The London Underground.

Twee - *adj* - Something that's quaint.

Twig - *v* - To catch on to something.

Twit – *n* - A foolish person.

Two up, two down - *n* - A house with two rooms downstairs and two rooms upstairs, popular in Victorian times.

Twonk - *n* - An idiot.

Tyke - *n* - A rascally child.

Tyre - *n* - How the British spell tire.

U

Ulcer – *n* - Canker sore.
Undercarriage - *n* - 1.
Male or female
genitals. 2. The
underside of your car.
Underdone – *adj* –
Undercooked, rare.
Underground - *n* -
Usually refers to the
London Underground
but there are other
underground subway
systems in the UK.
Under offer – *v* - For
sale.
Uni - *n* - Short for
University or College
University - *n* - Even if
they're going to a
college, the post-
secondary school part
of their educational
career is called
University. Going to
university, when I was
at university, etc.
Up for it - *phrs* - To be
up to doing something
- enthusiastic about it.
Up the duff - *v* - To be
pregnant.

Up the pole - *inf* –
Dead drunk.
Uphill gardener - *n* - A
homosexual, derog.

V

V&A – *acronym* – Victoria and Albert Musuem.

VAT - *acronym* - Value Added Tax. Essentially a 20% sales tax on pretty much everything.

Vacancy – *n* – Job opening.

Vacuum Flask – *n* – Thermos like bottle.

V.C. – *acronym* – Victoria Cross – the highest military distinction available.

Verge - *n* - Shoulder on the side of the road.

Vest - *n* - Piece of clothing worn under your shirt. What Americans would call a *tank top*.

Video - *n* - What the British called a VCR.

Village green - n - Common land at the center of a village where people can play Cricket or Football.

Vino - *n* - Poor quality inexpensive wine.

W

WAG - *Acronym* - Stands for 'Wives and Girlfriends' and is related to the women who are involved with Football players. Slightly derogatory as it indicates the type of woman attracted to that type of lifestyle.

W.C. - *n* - Watercloset, which is a lavatory.

Waffle - *n* - To ramble or waste time talking about a subject.

Waistcoat - *n* - A vest.

Wally - *n* - An unintelligent person.

Wank - *v* - To masturbate.

Wanker - *adj* - Literally someone who enjoys to masturbate but usually used as an insult for an arsehole. "You wanker!"

Wappy – *adj* – Stupid and irresponsible.

Washing up - *n* - To do the dishes.

Washing up liquid - *n* - Dishwashing soap.

Waster - *n* - A Time waster or lazy person.

Waste bin – *n* – Wastebasket.

Way out - *n* - An exit. Often used instead of the word exit.

Wazz – *v* – To urinate.

Wazzock - *n* - An idiot.

Wellingtons - *n* - A type of waterproof rubber boot commonly worn in the countryside. Shorthand version is 'wellies.'

Wedding tackle - *n* - Male genitalia.

Wendy house - *n* - A small children's playhouse.

West End – *n* – Theatre district in London. London's "Broadway."

Wheelie Bin – *n* – Trash can, usually with wheels on it.

Whinge - *v* - To moan or whine about something. You pronounce the g.

Whip round - *n* - A group collection of money used to buy a gift for someone.

Whitehall – *n* – Centre of government in the UK.

White van man - *n* - A general term for contractors or home repairmen who usually travel around in an unmarked white van.

Whittling - *v* - To urinate in public.

Whitworth - *n* - Someone keen on classic.

Wholemeal flour - *n* - Whole grain wheat flour.

Whovian - *n* - A fan of the British science fiction TV show *Doctor Who*.

W.I. – *acronym* – The Women's Institute.

Wicked - *adj* - Something really cool.

Wind - *n* - When one farts or has bad gas.

Windscreen - *n* - Windshield.

Wing - *n* - Car fender.

Wing Commander – *n* – Lieutenant colonel.

Wireless – *n* – Radio.

Wizard - *adj* - Something really cool.

Wobbler - *n* - A fit of anger. Typically preceded by the word "to throw", as in "to throw a wobbler."

Wobbly - *n* - Something that's not quite right.

Wog – *n* – A dark skinned foreigner; very offensive.

Wonga - *n* - Another word for Money from the African term.

Wonky - *adj* - Something that's not quite right, off balance or off kilter.

Woolly - *adj* - Something that's not well defined.

Workhouse – *n* – The Poorhouse.

WRAC – *acronym* – Women's Royal Army Corps.

Wren – *inf* – A member of the Women's Royal Naval Service (WRNS).

Wretch - *v* - To throw up/vomit.

Y

Y-fronts - *n* - Men's undergarments.

Yank - *n* - Generally how Brits like to refer to Americans.

Yeoman – *n* – Small farmer.

Yob - *n* - A young hooligan, usually identified by wearing a hood.

Yobbo – *n* – Lout or a bum, similar to yob.

Yonks - *n* - A long time.

Yummy Mummy - *n* - A young, good looking mother.

Z

Zapper - *n* - TV remote
control.

Zebra crossing - *n* -
Pedestrian crossings on
roads.

Zed - *n* - The British
pronounce the letter Z as
'zed.' They don't say
'zee.'

Time and Dates

The British do many things differently but one of the most fundamental differences is how they handle dates and time. It's different enough to confuse travelers and business people alike. So, here's a simple breakdown of the differences in dates and time with the British.

Dates

In America, we usually write the date as Month/Day/Year - February 1st, 2016 as an example.

In Britain, they write the date as Day/Month/Year - 1 February 2016 (they don't usually use st, th suffixes on dates either). This can get really confusing when the dates are just written at 1/2/2016 - which in American is 2/1/2016.

As a rule of thumb, always double check an important date if you're traveling to the UK so you don't end up on a train platform without a train or valid ticket because it's the wrong day.

In America, we usually start the week on Sunday. In Britain, the week usually starts on Monday. Which makes the word 'weekend' make a lot more sense.

Time

Speaking of trains, Britain follows the European convention of using 24-hour time for transport related timings (we call this Military time in the USA). This means instead of using a 12-hour clock, they use a 24-hour clock. You'll encounter this whenever you travel by Britain's rails or even use the airport. The most important thing to note is that if a time is under 12, then it's in the morning.

A simple rule of thumb for figuring out the time is to take the time, let's say 22:00 hours and simply subtract 12. That will give you 10 p.m. (NOT 10 a.m.).

Here's a handy translation chart:

00:00 / Midnight
01:00 / 1:00 a.m.
02:00 / 2:00 a.m.
03:00 / 3:00 a.m.
04:00 / 4:00 a.m.
05:00 / 5:00 a.m.
06:00 / 6:00 a.m.
07:00 / 7:00 a.m.
08:00 / 8:00 a.m.
09:00 / 9:00 a.m.
10:00 / 10:00 a.m.
11:00 / 11:00 a.m.
12:00 / 12:00 p.m.
13:00 / 1:00 p.m.
14:00 / 2:00 p.m.
15:00 / 3:00 p.m.
16:00 / 4:00 p.m.
17:00 / 5:00 p.m.
18:00 / 6:00 p.m.
19:00 / 7:00 p.m.
20:00 / 8:00 p.m.
21:00 / 9:00 p.m.
22:00 / 10:00 p.m.
23:00 / 11:00 p.m.

Now to make thing a little more confusing, in casual conversation and on Telly, they'll use the 12 hour clock. But even then, they do it differently. It's easier just to give a few examples.

"Let's meet at half 7 p.m."
Translation?
"Let's meet at 7:30 p.m."

"It's quarter past 10."
Translation?
"It's 10:15"

"It's a quarter to 10."
Translation?
"It's 9:45"

Weights & Measures

Britain is a hybrid country. It invented the system of Imperial measurements but they now mostly use the metric system. The key word there is mostly. As with all things British, it's more complicated but no worries, we're going to try and break it down for you.

Temperature

Britain uses the metric system for temperature measurement in all situations. For those not familiar, it's really simple but 0 degrees is freezing and 100 degrees is boiling. But where it gets confusing is when you're trying to read the weather forecast. Having to convert is a bunch of math that most people don't want to do. So, here's a quick breakdown of what those temperatures mean (with a little humor thrown in).

-10 Siberia
-5 Freezing your Bollocks Off
0 Cold
5 Do I Need a Coat?
10 Basically a Spring Day
15 Heatwave
20 Pleasant
25 A Real Heatwave (And you start to realize that AirCon isn't common in Britain)
30 Basically Dubai
35 Typical Southern USA Summer
40 The Face of the Sun

Weight

Now weights and measures are another matter. Officially Britain uses the metric system; in practice there are still a few holdouts.

The metric system is based on 10. For length:

10 millimeters (mm) = 1 centimeter (cm)
10 centimeters = 1 decimeter (dm) = 100 millimeters
100 centimeter = 1 meter (m) = 1,000 millimeters
1000 meters = 1 kilometer (km)

While this is the official system, in practice, speed is still measured in Imperial Miles, speedometers are in miles, but you buy gas by the litre. It's so odd really. Roads signs will all be written in miles as well.

Here is a breakdown for weight:

10 milligrams (mg) = 1 centigram (cg)
10 centigrams = 1 decigram (dg) = 100 milligrams
10 decigrams = 1 gram (g) = 1,000 milligrams
10 grams = 1 dekagram (dag)
10 dekagrams = 1 hectogram (hg) = 100 grams
10 hectograms = 1 kilogram (kg) = 1,000 grams
1,000 kilograms = 1 metric ton (t)

In practice you will mostly see weights broken down by grams or kilograms. However, there is a completely different weight the British used called 'Stone.' This is usually used when measuring the weight of a person. A stone is equal to 14 lbs or 6.3503 kilograms. A person would say they weigh 6 stone and that would translate to 84 lbs. It's an odd system.

Volume

Here is a breakdown for volume:

10 milliliters (ml) =   1 centiliter (cl)
10 centiliters =   1 deciliter (dl)   = 100 milliliters
10 deciliters =   1 liter (l)   = 1,000 milliliters
10 liters =   1 dekaliter (dal)
10 dekaliters =   1 hectoliter (hl)   = 100 liters
10 hectoliters =   1 kiloliter (kl)   = 1,000 liters

In practice you'll generally see liquids in milliliters, liters or kiloliters. Beer and Milk are the only things sold by the pint nowadays. FYI, a British pint is 20 fluid ounces compared to an American pint which is 16 fluid ounces.

English Currency

Pink Floyd once said that money is a gas, the Beatles said that it can't buy love, and others have said that it's what makes the world go 'round. British money pre-decimal gets a bit confusing, with many different types of coins representing fractions of pennies and larger currency. The official name for British money is the Pound Sterling, often referred to as simply the pound. While bills have tended to be fairly simple over the years, the coins that comprised a pound pre-decimalisation can get pretty complicated. Join us as we look at the history and breakdown of English money both before and after 1971.

After the Romans, Anglo-Saxon King Offa reintroduced an institutionalised monetary system in the 7th Century, producing coins that became the earliest silver pennies. These early pennies were made from pure silver, but by the reign of King Henry II, they were about 92.5% silver and the remainder included copper and other metals. These were dubbed the pound sterling. It wasn't necessarily a shortage of silver or cheapness that motivated the change, but the sterling silver coins proved to be much more durable and lasted longer in circulation.

The original Royal Mint, responsible for the manufacture of coins, dates back to Alfred the Great in 866 AD. In 1279, the mint moved to the Tower of London and remained there for another 500 years before branching out beyond the Tower to more modern buildings. During this time the first pound coin was produced in 1489 under King Henry VII. Banknotes, or what we think of as paper money, began to appear in 1694 and the earliest ones were hand-written. Sir Isaac Newton unofficially moved to the gold standard in 1717 when he was Master of the Royal Mint, and the gold standard would be adopted officially in the 19th Century after the value of silver decreased such that most coins contained only trace amounts of the metal. The Bank of England ultimately abandoned the gold standard in 1931.

The earliest breakdown of the pound divided it into shillings and pennies. One pound equaled 240 pennies and twelve pennies equaled one shilling. Pennies were further broken down when the halfpenny (also known as a ha'penny) and the farthing were introduced in the 13th Century, representing one-half and one-quarter of a penny, respectively. Another coin, the three farthings, had the value of 3/4 of a penny. Multiple penny (or "pence") coins were introduced later on, including the twopence, threepence, groat (worth four pence), and the sixpence.

From 1502 until decimalisation, the shilling (also known as a "bob") was worth twelve pence. After decimalisation, it became worth five pence until it was eventually phased out. A coin worth two shillings was known as a florin, while a half-crown was worth two shillings and sixpence. A crown was five shillings or 1/4 of a pound. Pound coins were often referred to as a sovereign, while a half-pound was known as a half-sovereign, both so named due to their tendency to have a portrait of the monarch on them. A larger coin was known as a guinea, often made out of gold from the Guinea coast of Africa and was worth one pound and one shilling. The largest coin in circulation for the most time was the five pounds, which remained in circulation until 1990.

In 1960, the British government set up the Committee of the Inquiry on Decimal Currency and on their recommendation, the British government set up the Decimal Currency Board to change over to a new system in which one pound would equal one-hundred pence. As part of the transition, certain coins were phased out of use, including halfpennies, half-crowns, and farthings. Everything switched over officially on 15 February 1971, known as "Decimal Day", though some shops and institutions used both for a limited time as people adjusted.

Under the decimal system, new coins were introduced that broke down into 1 pence, 2 pence, 5 pence, 10 pence, 20 pence (introduced in 1982), 50 pence, £1 (introduced in 1983), and £2 (introduced in 1997). While pre-decimal coins are not considered legal tender, the public outcry permitted the sixpence to continue use until 1980 and was worth 2.5p under the new system. One pound notes were also in circulation under the decimal system, but eventually ceased in England in 1988, though they are still issued by the Bank of Scotland and the Bank or Ireland. Other typical banknotes include £5, £10, £20, £50, and £100 (as well as larger amounts, though they are unlikely to be found in a billfold).

And that's the end of this primer on pre-and-post-decimal currency. While this only scratches the surface, there is plenty more information that goes into even greater detail concerning the history of English money and the many types of coins that have been available over the centuries. And of course, there's also the Euro to consider, but that's a topic for another time.

British Police Ranks

"Rank has its privileges" they say, and in any military or police organization you can find quite a lot of them. Ranks exist to create order and a clear chain of command between officers with different levels of experience. In the UK, ranks tend to be fairly standardized from jurisdiction to jurisdiction, with some minor differences. Watching any mystery show or police procedural, you may be a little lost trying to determine what's what. Well, have no fear, Anglotopia readers, because here is your guide to basic ranks of the British police services!

Police Constable

The lowest rank on the totem pole o the police service, the Police Constable (also called "PC") is the foot soldier in fight against crime. As such, they have the most direct contact with the people they serve at the local level, not just arresting baddies, but also conducting community outreach, collecting information at the scene, submitting reports, and working crowd control. On a programme, they're most often the officers who discover the initial crime, keeping onlookers from interfering with the scene, doing office work, or running errands for the higher ranking officers.

Sergeant

A Sergeant is the first supervisory rank and oftentimes the first "Detective" rank in many programmes. The rank is senior to "Constable" and junior to "Inspector". Sergeants are largely operational officers, both supervising constables and managing the day-to-day

administration of the division. Though the rank of
"Detective Constable" exists, these officers are mostly
training to become detectives, and often the first
detective rank you'll see in a programme is that of
"Detective Sergeant". These plain-clothed officers are
not necessarily superior to other Sergeants, but their rank
identifies them as members of the Criminal Investigative
Division (CID) or the Special Branch.

Inspector

Inspector is the second supervisory rank. Like Sergeants,
they are mainly concerned with operational duties, and a
uniformed Inspector is often responsible for supervising
a duty shift of Constables and Sergeants. Most
protagonist detectives in police programmes tend to be
this rank, including Inspector Endeavour Morse and
Detective Inspector Sam Tyler of "Life of Mars."

Chief Inspector

The next supervisory level, a Chief Inspector is the
senior officer in command of a district, usually of one or
more local authority areas. In a larger town, the rank has
often replaced that of Superintendent, such as Chief
Inspector Frank Butterman in the film "Hot Fuzz". A
Detective Chief Inspector tends to be the Senior
Investigating Officer in a CID branch. Notable examples
include DCI Gene Hunt from "Life on Mars" and "Ashes
to Ashes", DCI John Luther from "Luther", and DCI
Greg Lestrade from "Sherlock". Typically, these are the
highest officers one will see as a regular character.

Superintendent/Chief Superintendent

Every once in a while, the Superintendent will make an
appearance on a programme, if they are not already a
recurring character. In the past, Superintendents were in

charge of each division. A Detective Chief Superintendent is senior to the Detective Chief Inspector and the Detective Superintendent. A Chief Superintendent is the highest rank below the Chief Officer Level. Chief Superintendents will command the largest areas of supervision. The Detective Chief Superintendent is the highest rank possible in the CID, often serving as the senior detective and commanding officer.

Chief Officers

These highest-ranking officers are rarely seen in any police or mystery programme unless something very big is happening. A Commander is a chief officer rank for the City of London and the Metropolitan Police. They are senior to Chief Superintendents but junior to Deputy Assistant Commissioners. The Deputy Assistant Commissioner rank is equivalent to Deputy Chief Constable and Assistant Constable in forces outside of London. A Chief Constable is the chief officer for a territorial police force outside of London. The Deputy Commissioner, as you may imagine, is the second-in-command of London's Metropolitan Police Service, while the Commissioner is over the entirety of the City of London or the Metropolitan Police Service.

British Armed Forces Ranks

The military of any country is a vital part to keeping the people safe from external threats. In Britain before the 17th century, military forces were usually formed when there was a need to attack someone else or whenever the land itself came under attack, with the soldiers and sailors conscripted from the local populace. The English Army formed as a standing military force in 1660 and in 1707, the English and Scottish armies combined into one operational command. The first rank insignia for the British Army weren't introduced until 1760 and badges for field officers came about in 1810.

Army Ranks

For the most part, British ranks are very similar to their American counterparts, which is not surprising considering American ranks and military culture was based upon the British. The first enlisted rank is that of Private and actually has no insignia. The next up is Lance Corporal or Lance Bombardier (a Bombardier designating someone in artillery), followed by Corporal or Bombardier, with the former's insignia being one chevron and the latter having two chevrons. At three chevrons, one is designated a Sergeant. The next level up presents a difference as a Staff Sergeant has four chevrons and a crown. At this level, the Royal Marines designate this rank as a Colour Sergeant. The highest two enlisted ranks are Warrant Officer Class 2 and

Warrant Officer Class 1, the former includes a Quartermaster Sergeant. Class 2 rank insignia is a crown and for a Quartermaster Sergeant, a crown encircled with a laurel. Warrant Officer Class 1 insignia features the Royal Coat of Arms with a laurel as these warrant officers are appointed to the Royal Logistics Corps.

On the officer side, Officer Cadets are the first rank for Officer Candidates and have shoulder boards with a single white stripe across them. They are referred to as "Mister" or "Miss" rather than by rank and this is true for both the British Army and the Royal Air Force. The first rank of a commissioned officer is Second Lieutenant (pronounced *leftenant* by the British) and its insignia is a single Bath star (more commonly referred to as a "pip"). A Lieutenant has two pips and a Captain has three pips. At the rank of Major, the insignia is a single St. Edward's Crown, while a Lieutenant Colonel has one crown and one pip. Colonel has a crown and two pips and a Brigadier has a crown and three pips. After that, you get into the General ranks, with the first being a Major General whose insignia features a pip over a crossed sword and baton. A Lieutenant General keeps the sword and baton, but the pip is replaced with a crown. A full General has all three symbols: Crown, pip, and sword and baton. At the top is a Field Marshal, an appointed position that is designated by a crown over two crossed batons on a red field surrounded by yellow leaf. On appointment, a Field Marshal receives a gold-tipped baton that he must carry with him on formal occasions.

Royal Navy Ranks

Meanwhile, despite the fact that they were both formed in 1660, the Royal Navy's formation before the Army's designates it as the "Senior Service". As stated, Royal Marines, even though they are part of the Navy, have roughly the same ranks as the Army. Enlisted sailors' ranks begin with Able Seaman with an insignia that simply says "Royal Navy". The next rank is Leading Rate, the insignia of which features an anchor. Following that is the rank of Petty Officer, which features a crown over two crossed anchors. A Chief Petty Officer, meanwhile, features a crown over an anchor encircled with a gold leaf. Lastly, much like the Warrant Officer classes for the Army, Class 2 features a crown inside a gold leaf while Class 1 also has the Royal Coat of Arms.

Naval officers begin with Officer Cadet at the Britannia Royal Naval College before formal training begins, then ascend to the rank of Midshipmen for the remainder of their time at the college. Their first rank on graduation is Sub Lieutenant and the insignia features one gold braid stripe with an executive curl. A Lieutenant features this curl with an additional gold stripe under it, while a Lieutenant Commander has both a thin gold stripe as well as a medium stripe. A full Commander has the curl with two medium stripes and a Captain has the curl and three medium stripes. Meanwhile, a Commodore's insignia features a gold loop with a very wide gold lace stripe. At the Admiralty level, a Rear Admiral's sleeve features the executive curl with the wide stripe, while also having shoulder boards with a crown and sword and crossed baton over two stars. A Vice Admiral is similar but with three stars and an Admiral has four stars, while their sleeves include a curl and wide stripe with one and two medium stripes, respectively. Lastly, Admiral of the Fleet, much like Field Marshal, features a crown over a sword and crossed baton encircled with silver leaf, while the sleeves have a curl, wide stripe, and three medium stripes.

Royal Air Force

The Royal Air Force was founded in 1918 and is the most junior service. Its enlisted ranks begin with Aircraftman/woman which has no insignia, while the next rank up, Leading Aircraftman/woman features a two-bladed propeller. Next is Senior Aircraftman/woman which features a three-bladed propeller and if one is a Senior Aircraftman/woman Technician, the propeller is encased in a circle. Chevrons begin to be used at the rank of Lance Corporal, which features one chevron, followed by Corporal at two. Sergeants get three, but depending on rank and position, may include an eagle for Sergeant Aircrew, a four-bladed propeller for Chief Technician, and a crown for Flight Sergeant with an eagle added for Flight Sergeant Aircrew. Warrant Officers are same as in other services.

For Air Force Officers, an Acting Pilot Officer has one thin light blue stripe flanked by two black stripes until APO is regarded to Pilot Officer, which has the name insignia. The next rank, Flying Officer, receives a thicker medium stripe. A Flight Lieutenant receives two medium stripes, while a Squadron Leader has two medium stripes with a thin stripe between them. Moving up the chain, a Wing Commander has three medium stripes and a Squadron Commander has four. Air Commodore is the first to have a thick stripe, Air Vice Marshal has a thick stripe and one medium stripe, while Air Marshal has a thick stripe and two medium stripes, and Air Chief Marshal has three medium stripes. Lastly, the Marshal of the Royal Air Force, the top position in the RAF, has a thick stripe with four medium stripes as well as shoulder boards featuring an eagle surrounded by a wreath, two crossed marshal's batons, and a crown above it all.

The Peerage

In Britain, the peerage comprises a number of legal hereditary, life, and representative titles. The system dates back to the 11th Century and the Anglo-Saxons. It began as a means to protect England from invaders, with earls being appointed over various shires, which continued after the Norman conquest, though the administrative duties shifted to appointed sheriffs. Over time, a series of various titles evolved, including: Duke/Duchess, Marquess/Marchioness, Earl/Countess, Viscount/Viscountess, and Baron/Baroness.

Further, there are five co-existing peerages. The three oldest are the peerages of England, Scotland, and Ireland. With the Acts of Union of 1707, the English and Scottish peerages became the Peerage of Great Britain. After the Acts of Union of 1801, future peerages were made under the Peerage of the United Kingdom, including those from Ireland and now Northern Ireland. Traditionally, most of these peerages have been hereditary.

In the past, a hereditary peerage could only pass from fathers to sons. If the peer had no children, the title would pass to his brother. If he only had a daughter, it would pass to her husband. To this day, women are still not entitled to inherit most hereditary peerages. At one point, there were over 800 hereditary peers in the UK and a majority of them were entitled to sit in the House of Lords. However, under Tony Blair's government, the

House of Lords Act 1999 removed all but 92 of these seats.

The Life Peerage Act of 1958 created titles that only last for the life of the person appointed. The Prime Minister typically appoints life peers from his or her own party, though he or she may also appoint life peers from the opposition. These peers are expected to attend sessions of the House of Lords and they now make up the majority of the seats in the chamber. Representative peers, on the other hand, are peers chosen by the peers of Scotland and Ireland to represent those nations in the House of Lords. These peers were introduced after the Acts of Union 1707 and ended for Ireland when it became a free state in 1922, while Scottish peers continued until 1963 when all Scottish peers were permitted to sit in the House of Lords. The remaining representative peers were among the ninety-two hereditary peers under the 1999 act.

Duke/Duchess

King Edward III created the first dukedoms of Cornwall, Lancaster, and Clarence in 1337. Dukes are the highest rank of peerage below the sovereign. At present, there are roughly 30 dukedoms in the United Kingdom, with 10 of them being Royal Dukedoms, which are held by members of the Royal Family. For non-royal dukes, the rank goes in order of creation, meaning that the oldest non-royal duke is the most senior. The form of address for most dukes and duchesses is "Your Grace".

Marquess/Marchioness

King Richard II created the first Marquess when he appointed Robert de Vere, 9th Earl of Oxford, as the first Marquess of Dublin in 1385. The title of marquess is below a duke, but one level higher than an earl. King

George V styled most of his relatives as Marquess after they relinquished their German titles during World War I and the last Marquess created was the Marquess of Willingdon is 1936. No other such titles have been created since, with the most recent honour above an earl being the Duke and Duchess of Cambridge in 2011. A marquess or machioness is addressed as "The Most Honourable" or "My Lord Marquess/Madam".

Earl/Countess

As mentioned, "earl" is the oldest form of peerage dating back to pre-Norman times. The Norman equivalent was a Count, though that was not continued under King William I. However, the female title of countess is a holdover from the Normans. After William, succeeding kings continued to reduce the power of earls. Even so, they still had enough power to depose King Edward II. Over time, the earldoms came to be less associated with shires and more with towns, local landmarks, or surnames. The proper address for earls and countesses is "The Right Honourable Earl/Countess" and "My Lord/Madam".

Viscount/Viscountess

The fourth rank in the British peerage system, a viscount or viscountess is typically named in association with a place. The title originated under the Carolingians in France and was carried over to Britain by the Normans, though the use of it wasn't recorded until 1440, when King Henry VI created John Beaumont as Viscount Beaumont. It was a title created by the monarch and while it was similar to a life peerage at first, eventually it became a hereditary peerage. Viscounts and vicountesses are often addressed as "My Lord" or "Madam" rather than by their title.

Baron/Baroness

Baron or baroness is the lowest rank of peerage and were created by the Normans as a mostly administrative position within the "barony", or feudal tenure. In Scotland, the title became that of "thane", prominently remembered now from the play Macbeth. Barons were expected to be loyal to the king and serve as military commanders at the monarch's command. It was the barons who forced King John I to sign the Magna Carta and it was the barons who formed the first parliament. Over time, baronies became less tied to land and more products of royal creation. Further, all of the above titles also typically carry the title of baron. The proper title is typically "Lord" or "Lady" and the form of address is "My Lord" or "Madam."

Of course, this information represents only the basics of the peerage system and it is, in practice, very complex with a rich history and we have inevitably left some things out - this is meant to be a primer. There is plenty of information around the internet of you want to delve deeper into the intricacies of the British peerage system.

Honours System

We thought it would be fun to explore the British Honours system and what exactly it means to be called a Sir or Dame or get an MBE or OBE. As with anything British, it has a long history and can be a little confusing.

In the United Kingdom, the Queen is the "Fountain of Honour" and is responsible for recognising the achievements of men and women across the Commonwealth. The honours may be awarded for achievements in science, math, the arts, charity, and other activities that benefit the kingdom. Queen Elizabeth II typically awards honours twice a year, once on New Year's Day and again on her official birthday in June. Birthday Honours have been around since 1865, while New Year's Honours have been awarded since 1890, both begun during the reign of Queen Victoria and carried on by her successors.

There are different processes for selecting honours. The first and most common means is to make a recommendation to the Cabinet Office and the recommendations are managed by the Honours Committee. Nominations may be submitted by government departments or members of the public. Various government agencies then pour over each candidate to determine his or her suitability for the award. The Queen will then informally approve the list and award letters will be sent to the nominees. Once the nominees have accepted, the list of honours is finalised and published in the London Gazette.

The second and less common means is for the monarch to confer honours personally, which is reserved mostly for chivalric honours. These include: the Order of the Garter, the Order of the Thistle, the Order of Merit, the Royal Victorian Order and the Royal Victorian, the Royal Medal of Honour, and the Royal Medal for Long Service. The orders of chivalry are made on a personal order of the Queen and, in some cases, may be granted on special days separate from New Year's or the official birthday.

When it comes to the Orders of Knighthood, the first and most prominent is the Most Noble Order of the Garter. This is the oldest chivalric order, founded by King Edward III in 1348. The reason for its selectiveness is that the order is limited to the Sovereign, the Prince of Wales, and twenty-four "Knights Companion" or "Ladies Companion". There are also supernumerary members who do not count towards the twenty-four, which includes members of the Royal Family who are designated "Royal Knights and Ladies of the Garter". Foreign dignitaries may also be included in the order and are known as "Stranger Knights and Ladies of the Garter."

Second comes the Most Ancient and Noble Order of the Thistle, which was founded by King James II (VII of Scotland) and relates primarily to Scotland, and the Garter relates more to England and Wales. As with the Order of the Garter, the Order of the Thistle is a limited one reserved for the Sovereign and sixteen Knights and Ladies, who are known as "Knights and Ladies of the Thistle." There are also an unlimited number of "extra" knights and ladies. The order was suspended after James II was deposed in the Glorious Revolution, but revived with Queen Anne. This is the last order that invests women with the title of "Lady", with lower orders instead using the title "Dame".

Since the Order of St. Patrick has long since fallen dormant, the next chivalric order in precedence is the Most Honourable Order of the Bath, which was founded in 1725 by King George I. The name itself doesn't come from the City of Bath, but from the ancient method of awarding knighthood that required the candidate to bathe as part of the ceremony. The order has three grades and absolutely limits the number of members, with "Knight/Dame Grand Cross" set at 120 members, "Knight/Dame Commander" at 355, and "Companion" at 1,925 (Companions are not considered knights or dames). Further, while the Order of the Garter and Order of the Thistle are at the Sovereign's own selection, the Order of Bath is the first on which the nominations are made on the recommendation of the government.

The Most Distinguished Order of St. Michael and St. George, which is awarded primarily to diplomats, also has three levels of "Knight/Dame Grand Cross" (125 members), "Knight/Dame Commander" (375 members), and "Companion" (1,750 members). It was created by the Prince Regent, later King George IV, in 1818 and recognises the contributions of those who work overseas. Foreigners may be appointed as "honourary" members, but despite this status, they are still considered full members of the order. Another order dedicated to service is that of the Royal Victorian Order, which is awarded to persons for service to the Crown. It ties for the most grades of any order at five: 1) Knight/Dame Grand Cross, 2) Knight/Dame Commander, 3) Commander, 4) Lieutenant, and 5) Member. Since Queen Victoria created the order in 1896, it remains one of the only honours that is personally granted by the

Sovereign and does not require recommendation from the Cabinet.

One of the most publicly known chivalric honours is that of the Most Excellent Order of the British Empire. King George V founded it in 1917 as he realised that no specific honour existed for ordinary citizens who rendered great service to the British Empire. As such, this is the largest of the orders as the most public honours are admitted to this order, with thousands of people admitted every year. The Order of the British Empire is divided into two types: recognition for public service and recognition for military service. As with the Royal Victorian Order, it has five grades: 1) Knight/Dame Grand Cross, 2) Knight/Dame Commander, 3) Commander, 4) Officer, and 5) Member.

There are further honours that may be granted, though they confer no title. The Order of Merit acts similarly to the Order of the British Empire in that it may be rewarded for services in the arts or the military. The Distinguished Service Order is granted to administrative and clerical workers on the completion of twenty-five years of public service. The Distinguished Service Order is presented to military officers in wartime for meritorious or distinguished service. The Victoria Cross is the highest military award a member of the armed forces can receive and is forged of metal recast from Russian canons that were captured during the Crimean War. Meanwhile, St. George's Cross is the highest decoration for civilians, awarded for "acts of the greatest heroism or of the most conspicuous courage in circumstances of extreme danger."

While this is by no means the extent of the honours one may receive, the orders and awards covered above represent a wealth of distinguished service to Britain. Twice a year, these people receive the acknowledgment they so richly deserve. The men and women recognised by the Crown and the Government of the United Kingdom have helped to protect the county, nurture its culture, and serve its people.

British Insults

While we generally covered what is and isn't an insult in the main dictionary, we thought it'd be useful for quick reference to summarize all our favorite insults in one place. This is not an exhaustive list by any means.

Tosser - Supreme asshole or jerk.
Wanker - Idiot or someone who enjoys to masturbate.
Slag - Whore, the worst kind.
Cheese Eating Surrender Monkeys - The French.
Lost the plot - Gone crazy or completely stupid.
Daft Cow - Dumb, large woman.
Arsehole - Asshole.
Barmy - Stupid or crazy.
Chav - Low Class trash.
Dodgy - Something that's shady or doesn't work well.
Git - Moron, Idiot.
Gormless - Complete lack of common sense.
Manky - Disgusting.
Minger - Very unattractive woman.
Muppet - Dimwit (not the puppet variety).

Naff - Tacky.
Nutter - Someone's who's clearly crazy.
Pikey - Used to slight Gypsies or Irish Travellers.
Pillock - Idiot.
Plonker - Idiot.
Prat - Idiot, asshole.
Scrubber - A nicer way to say slag.
Trollop - A lady of questionable morals.
Uphill Gardener - Another way of saying homosexual.
Twit - Idiot.
Knob Head - Dickhead.
Piss Off - Go Away.
Bell End - Dick Head (bell end also means penis).
Lazy Sod - Useless idiot.
Skiver - Lazy sod.
Knob - Dick.

Wazzock - Someone so dumb they can only do manual labor (from Yorkshire).

Ninny - Brilliant but inferior.

Berk - Idiot.

Airy-fairy - Not strong, weak.

Ankle-biters - Children.

Arse-licker - A sycophant.

Arsemonger - A person that generate contempt.

Chuffer - An annoying perfusion.

Daft as a bush - Silly, Crazy.

Dead from the neck up - Stupid.

Gannet - Greedy person.

Gone to the dogs - rotten, deteriorated.

Ligger - Freeloader.

Like a dog with two dicks - Man whore.

Mad as a bag of ferrets - Crazy.

Maggot - A despicable person.

Mingebag - A bad person, an asshole who might be chcap.

Not batting on a full wicket - Eccentric person. a little crazy or odd.

Plug-Ugly - Very Ugly person.

London Slang

One thing you'll notice when you travel to London is all the different words they use to describe things. Sometimes they make sense, sometimes they don't. We thought it would be useful to put together a list of words you'll usually only hear in London. So, here's your guide to some useful London Lingo.

Tube - London Underground Network.

The Knowledge - The cumulative knowledge of London's black cab drivers that they have to learn to be licensed. They have to learn every street in London.

BoJo - Boris Johnson, the former mayor of London and current British Foreign Secretary.

Boris Bike - The bikes located in various places around London that you can rent by the half hour.

Boris Bus - Boris Johnson's key platform of replacing the old London Routemaster bus.

Red Ken - The name of London's former Mayor Ken Livingston who leaned VERY far to the left.

The Standard - Officially called the London Evening Standard - the evening paper dedicated to London.

The City - The City of London - the square mile bit of central London that goes back 2 thousand years.

Square Mile - Physical boundary of the City of London.

Congestion Charge - Tax on all cars entering the central London congestion charge zone.

Silicon Roundabout -
Area around Old Street
that's a hub for new
media and tech
companies.

Council Estate - Public
housing.

The Blitz - Period
between 1940 and 1941
when London was
bombed by the Nazis.

M25 - The Orbital
Highway that encircles
London.

Westway - Elevated
Highway in West
London.

Mind the Gap - Watch
your step when stepping
from a train to a platform
on the Tube.

The Palace - When
someone says the Palace
they're almost always
referring to Buckingham
Palace, the Queen's
official residence in
London.

Buck House -
Buckingham Palace.

The Tower - Tower of
London.

A-Z - A popular London
map guide that's
indispensable to locals
and long term visitors
(extra note - Londoners
will say 'A to Zed').

GMT - Greenwich Mean
Time.

Cockney - Someone born
within earshot of the
bells of St Mary-le-Bow.

Offy - Convenience Store
that also sells alcohol.

Off License -
Convenience Store that
also sells alcohol.

Take Away - Cheap food
to go.

Crossrail - New cross
London underground
railway line currently
under construction.

Bobby - London
Policeman

Clip Joint - A club that
claims to be a strip club
but usually comes with
£100 bottles of water.
Avoid.

Zebra Crossing -
Pedestrian crossing.

Home Counties - Generic name for the counties around London which are: Bedfordshire, Berkshire, Buckinghamshire, Cambridgeshire, Dorset, Essex, Hampshire, Hertfordshire, Kent, Middlesex, Oxfordshire, Surrey and Sussex.

Nappy Valley - Areas of London with high birthrates like Battersea.

The Big Smoke - Another term for London.

Oyster Card - A electronic card used to pay for the Tube without a paper ticket. Often you get a cheaper fare this way.

London Street Slang

English is a forever evolving language. It changes the most on the streets of London as the various ethnicities that have settled in London co-mingle their native languages with English. Interesting things result from this. There are new words all the time, old words are brought back into fashion, some words now mean the opposite of what they used to mean. It's all very fascinating and confusing to visitors as well!

Here are a few new words that have made their way into the current London Urban vernacular. Some of them may still have you scratching your head. And the meaning may completely change by tomorrow morning!

Peng - N - Excellent, very good, attractive. Popularised on the streets of London in the ethnic neighborhoods. "She is so Peng." "Or that food was the Pengest munch."

Peak - Adj - One would think this would be an adjective to describe something grand, it actually means the exact opposite. "There's a rail strike again this weekend; it's so peak".

Bossman - N - Used to refer to a shopowner or someone working in the service industry. Like the person serving you chicken at the local chippie. "'Ello Bossman, I'll have four thighs."

Mandem - N - A group of acquaintances that aren't as cool as they think, slightly ropey. "Oh looks like the mandem are hanging out a the skate park again."

Roadman - N - That intimidating, slightly sketchy looking character who knows the neighborhood better than anyone. Probably the person to ask for direction. "What? Does he think he's some kind of roadman?"

Northerner - N - Anyone who lives outside the M25 ring road that surrounds London. "I think he's a Northerner."

Blower - N - The phone. "Hey mate, your dad's on the blower."

Lit - Adj - Something that is exciting or big bash. "Man, that party was lit!"

Dench - Adj - Someone who has bulked themselves up successfully. "You are so dench now that you have been down the gym."

Wavey - Adj - To be drunk or high on drugs. "He was so wavey at the party last night."

In Ends - N - Your local area. "I've been in ends all day, mate."

Link - V - To meet up with friends or hang out. "Don't forget to link up with us later."

Chirpsing - V - Casual flirting. "He was over there chirpsing with the girls."

Choong - N - Good looking, attractive. "Oh man, he was soooo choong."

Tekker - N - Someone with great technical ability. "Hey, take this over to the tekkers down the street to get it fixed."

Vex - Adj - Angry. "I heard her on the phone earlier; she was vex."

Reh teh teh - Adj - A phrase that basically means etc.

Looking criss - Adj - Looking fresh, sharp. "I saw her coming out of the hairdressers and she was looking criss."

Kicks - N - A pair of American style sneakers (normally called trainers in England). "Did you see his beautiful new kicks?"

Tea Related Words

Tea is a culture entirely of its own in Britain. It's not a stereotype; most Brits really do love their tea and cherish a cuppa. It's a form of relaxation and socialization that is key to 'getting' Britain (like talking about the weather). But there is a lot of confusion out there - many people don't realize the difference between High Tea or Afternoon Tea or Cream Tea. So, here's a short list to help translate the differences.

Cuppa - Your simple cup of tea at any time of the day.

Elevensies - Late morning snack and cup of tea (second breakfast).

Afternoon Tea - A Formal meal where one sits down with cucumber sandwiches, pastries, and fine tea. Usually in a hotel or restaurant around 4 pm.

High Tea - Less formal than afternoon Tea - usually a late afternoon meal after work but before proper dinner.

Cream Tea - A simpler tea service consisting of tea, scones, clotted cream, marmalade or lemon curd.

Royale Tea - Tea service with champagne or sherry at the end.

Celebration Tea - An afternoon tea service where a cake is served for a special occasion.

Kettle - Where you boil water to make tea. Many Brits will use an electric kettle (which boil water very fast).

Cockney Rhyming Slang

Cockney Rhyming Slang is believed to have originated in the mid-19th century in the East End of London, with sources suggesting sometime in the 1840s. The Cockney population are well-known for having a characteristic accent and speech patterns.

It remains a matter of speculation whether rhyming slang was a linguistic accident, a game, or a secret language developed intentionally to confuse non-locals. If deliberate, Cockneys may also have used it to maintain a sense of community. It is possible that it was used in the marketplace to allow vendors to talk amongst themselves in order to facilitate collusion, without customers knowing what they were saying. Another suggestion is that criminals may have been used it to confuse the police.

What follows is a list of words that rhyme, but also a list of words commonly used by Cockney speakers.

A

Adam and Eve - Believe.

Afters - Short for the term 'after hours'.

Agro - Short for violence.

Alan Whicker(s) - Rhyming Slang for 'knickers'.

All over the gaff/shop - Someone that's in a mess.

Allright / awright - Greeting that means 'is everything all right?'

Apples and pears - Stairs.

Artful Dodger - Lodger.

Ascot Races - Braces.

Aunt Joanna - Piano.

Ayrton Senna - Rhyming Slang for 'tenner'.

B

Backhander - A dodgy payment.

Baked Bean - Queen.

Baker's Dozen - Cousin.

Ball and Chalk - Walk.

Ballistic - To go mad.

Banged up - To be put in prison.

Bangers - Another name for sausages.

Banjaxed - Meaning drunk or stoned.

Barmy - A mad person.

Barnaby Rudge - Judge.

Barnet Fair - Hair.

Barney - Violent argument.

Barney Rubble - Trouble.

Battlecruiser - Boozer.

Bean flicker - A lesbian.

Beer monster - A laddish heavy drinker.

Bees and honey - Money.

Bell - A telephone call.

Bender - A drinking spree, or a gay bloke.

Bent - Stolen.

Bent as a nine bob note - Illegal.

Bimbo - A young woman considered sexually attractive but of limited intelligence.

Bird lime - Time in prison.

Bit of awright - Used by men to refer to an attractive young lady.

Blinder - Amazing or wonderful.

Blow-off - Fart.

Blower - Slang for telephone.

Bluey - Pornographic video.

Bo Peep - Rhyming Slang for 'sleep'.

Boat Race - Face.

Bob Hope - Rhyming Slang for 'dope'.

Borasic lint - Rhyming Slang for 'skint'.

Bottle - Courage.

Bottle and glass - Arse.

Botty boy - Offensive slang for gay man.

Bovver - Fighting.

Brahms and Liszt - Pissed (drunk).

Brass Tacks - Facts.

Bread - Rhyming slang for 'money'.

Bread and Cheese - Sneeze.

Bread and Honey - Money.

Bricks and Mortar - Daughter.

Bristol City - Breasts.

Brown Bread - Dead.

Bubble and Squeak - Greek.

Bubble Bath Laugh.

Bun in the oven - Meaning pregnant.

Bunk-off - To be absent without permission.

Bunk-up - Sexual intercourse.

Butcher's hook - A look.

C

Cabbage - Bit slow or foolish.

Cabbaged - Used for tired of drunk.

Cack - Rubbish.

Cakehole - Mouth.

Caned - Drunk or stoned.

Carpet muncher - Lesbian.

Chalfont St. Giles - Piles.

Chalk Farm - Arm.

Char / cha - Tea.

Charlie - Cocaine.

Chief - Used to address a man.

China - Rhyming Slang, short for 'China plate', 'mate'.

China plate - Mate (friend).

Chip - To leave.

Choked - Very disappointed.

Chronic - Terrible.

Chutney ferret - Gay man.

Claire Rayner's - Rhyming Slang for 'trainers'.

Claret - Slang for blood.

Cobblers - Rhyming Slang, short for 'cobblers awls', 'balls'.

Cock and bull story - A rubbish story.

Cock and Hen - Ten.

Cop shop - Police station.

Cows and Kisses - Missus (wife).

Crack - Something that is a laugh.

Crikey - Astonishment.

Crust - Money.

Currant bun - Sun (also The Sun, a British newspaper).

Custard and jelly - Telly (television).

D

Daisy Roots - Boots.

Darby and Joan - Moan.

Dead cert - Definite.

Diamond geezer - A reliable person.

Dicky bird - Word.

Dicky Dirt - Shirt.

Diesel dyke - A butch lesbian.

Diggs - Lodgings.

Ding-dong - Argument.

Dinky Doos - Shoes.

Dodgy - Dubious person.

Dog and bone - Phone.

Dog's dinner - Overdressed.

Dog's meat - Feet [from early 20th c.].

Done over - Beaten up.

Doris - A woman who is plain.

Dosh - Money.

Dosser - Tramp.

Double bubble - Double time.

Duck and Dive - Skive.

Duke of Kent - Rent.

Dustbin lid - Kid.

E

Elephant's Trunk - Drunk.

Emma Freud's - Rhyming Slang for hemorrhoids.

Extracting the urine - Taking the piss.

F

Family jewels - Rhyming Slang for 'balls'.

Farmer Giles - Rhyming Slang for 'piles'.

Fireman's Hose - Nose.

Float an air biscuit - To fart.

Flowery Dell - Cell.

Folding - Paper money.

Fridge and freezer - Rhyming Slang for 'geezer'.

Frog and Toad - Road.

Funny farm - Mental hospital.

Funny money - Counterfeit money.

G

Geezer - A man.

Ginger beer - Rhyming Slang for queer.

Gone for a Burton - Rhyming Slang for 'to leave'.

Goolies - Balls, testicles.

Gooner - An Arsenal fan.

Goppin' - Ugly or disgusting in some way.

Gordon Bennet - An exclamation.

Got the nod - To receive approval.

Gregory Peck - Rhyming Slang for 'neck'.

Guv'nor or guv - Meaning 'boss'.

Gypsy's kiss - Piss.

H

Hacked off - Fed up, annoyed.

Had it away on his toes - To run away quickly.

Half-inch - Pinch (to steal).

Hammered - Drunk.

Hampstead Heath - Rhyming Slang for 'teeth'.

Hampton Wick - Prick.

Hank Marvin - Starving.

Herbert - A foolish person.

Hole in the wall - Cashpoint machine.

Holy Ghost - Rhyming Slang for 'toast'.

How's your father - A euphemism for sex.

I

In stook - In trouble.

Irish pig - Wig.

Isle of Wight - Tights.

J

Jack Jones - Rhyming Slang for 'own'.

Jam-jar - Car.

Jazz mag - Pornographic magazine.

Jimmy Riddle - Piddle.

Joanna - Piano (pronounced 'pianna' in Cockney).

Johnny-bag - Condom.

Juiced / juiced up - Very drunk.

K

Keep your hair on - Keep calm.
Khyber Pass - Arse.
Kick and Prance - Dance.
Kick it off - Start a fight.
Knocking shop - Brothel.

L

Lady Godiva - Fiver.
Laugh n a joke - Smoke.
Leave it out - Stop doing that.
Leg-over - To have sexual intercourse.
Leggit - Run away fast.
Legless - Very drunk.
Lionel Blairs - Flares.
Loaf of Bread - Head.
Loop the loop - Soup.
Lost the plot - Gone crazy/mad.
Luvvly jubbly - That all is well.

M

Manor - Territory, area, turf.
Mickey Bliss - Piss.
Mince Pies - Eyes.
Minging - Drunk, disgusting.

Missus - Bit of a lad's term for the wife.
Nonkey - A term for £500.
Moolar - A slang term for money of uncertain origin.
Mork and Mindy - Windy'.
Motor / motah - A car.
Mug / muggins - A fool or victim.
Muppet - A foolish or stupid person.
Mutt 'n Jeff - Rhyming Slang for deaf.
Mystic Meg(s) - Rhyming Slang - for 'legs'.

N

Nadds, nadgers - Testicles.
Naff - Cheap and nasty.
Naff off - "Go away".
Night out on the tiles - A late night out, usually drunk.
Nipper - A small child.
Nonce - A sex offender.
North and south - Mouth.
Notes - A term used to mean money in general.
Nugget - A pound coin.

O

Off your face - To be drunk.

Off your trolley / rocker - A bit mad, crazy.

Oily (rag) - Rhyming Slang for cigarette.

Old fruit - An affectionate address.

On the game - To be prostitute.

On the job - To be involved in sexual activity.

Orchestra stalls - Balls.

Out of your tree - Crazy, drunk or stoned.

P

Pan handle - An erection.

Pat and Mick - Sick.

Pear-shaped - It has gone wrong.

Peckham Rye - Tie.

Pen and ink - Rhyming Slang for 'stink'.

Pete Tong - Rhyming Slang for 'wrong'.

Pictures of the Queen - Paper money.

Plates of meat - Feet.

Pony - Slang term for £25.

Pony and Trap - Crap.

Porky pies - Rhyming Slang for 'lies'.

Powder your nose - Taking cocaine.

R

Rabbit (rabbit and pork) - Rhyming Slang for 'talk'.

Radio Rental - Rhyming Slang for 'mental'.

Raspberry ripple - Nipple.

Raspberry tart - Fart.

Rat-arsed - Drunk.

Roast Pork - Fork.

Rosy Lee - Tea (drink).

Round the Houses - Trousers.

Rub-a-Dub - Pub.

Ruby Murray - Curry.

Rug - Wig, toupee.

S

Sausage Roll - Goal.

Scarpa / scarper - Rhyming Slang for 'to run off'.

Scrounge - To beg or sponge.

Septic tank - Yank.

Sexton Blake - Rhyming Slang for 'fake'.

Shagged-out - To feel tired.

Shed-load - A huge amount.

Shell-like - The ear.

Shell-out - To have to pay for

Sherbert dab - Rhyming Slang for 'cab'

Skin and Blister - Sister

Skin diver - Rhyming Slang for 'fiver'

Skint - To have no money

Skirt - Young attractive woman.

Sky Rocket - Pocket

Spliff - Common term for a cannabis cigarette.

Spondulics - Money.

Steffi (Graff) - Rhyming Slang for 'laugh'.

Steve Mcqueen's - Rhyming Slang for 'bake beans'.

Stuffing - To perform sexual intercourse.

Stunner - A very good looking bird.

Sweeney Todd - Flying squad.

Syrup of figs - Wig (sic).

T

Tables and chairs - Stairs.

Tea leaf - Thief.

That old chestnut - See chestnut.

The nick - Police station, or prison.

Thrupenny bits - Rhyming Slang for 'tits'.

Tits-up - All gone wrong.

To go down - Sent to prison.

Todd Sloane - Alone.

Tom and Dick - Sick.

Tomfoolery - Jewelry.

Tommy Trinder - Window.

Trouble and strife - Wife.

Trouser action - A general euphemism for sexual activity.

Two and eight - State (of upset).

U

Uncle Tom Cobley and all - Everyone.

V

Vera Lynn - Gin.

W

Weasel and stoat -
Rhyming Slang for
'coat'.
Well ard/hard - Someone
or something that is very
tough.
Whistle and flute - Suit
(of clothes).
Wind up - To tease, to
perform a prank.
Wind-up merchant -
Someone who
specializes in teasing.
Wonga - Money.

Christmas Words

While the basics of the holiday season in Britain are pretty much the same as anywhere else in the English speaking world, there are key differences and many of them are easily defined by the words used to name them. So, we present here a list of words related to British Christmas to help you understand how the Brits celebrate the holiday season (which for them includes Christmas, Boxing Day and New Year's). This will be quite handy when you watch any British Telly Christmas specials.

Boxing Day

Boxing Day is a holiday that's the day after Christmas. Traditionally it's when servants and tradesmen would receive gifts, known as a "Christmas box", from their bosses or employers. It hasn't been that for a long time now - it's now just another 'Bank Holiday' (see this for what that is) which means most people get the day off. Except for the poor unfortunate souls working the Boxing Day sales which are roughly equivalent to 'Black Friday' in the USA. Many folks will also have a special Boxing Day lunch featuring a special meal or leftovers from the Christmas feast the day before.

Twelfth night

Twelfth Night is a festival marking the coming of the Epiphany, the day when the nativity story tells us that the three wise men visited the infant Jesus. Different traditions mark the date of Twelfth Night on either 5 January or 6 January; the Church of England celebrates Twelfth Night on January 5th and "refers to the night before Epiphany, the day when the nativity story tells us that the three wise men visited the infant Jesus". In the UK this is the unofficial end of the holiday season and when many people shuffle back to work. It's also when people usually take down their Christmas trees and decorations. A belief has arisen in modern times, in some English-speaking countries, that it is unlucky to leave Christmas decorations hanging after Twelfth Night.

Hogmanay

Aka Scottish New Year's. Hogmanay is the Scots word for the last day of the year and is synonymous with the celebration of the New Year (Gregorian calendar) in the Scottish manner. It is normally followed by further celebration on the morning of New Year's Day (1 January) or, in some cases, 2 January—a special Scottish Bank Holiday. The origins of Hogmanay are unclear, but may be derived from Norse and Gaelic observances. Customs vary throughout Scotland, and usually include gift-giving and visiting the homes of friends and neighbours, with special attention given to the first-foot, the first guest of the new year.

Christmas Specials

One of the most well known traditions during Christmas is when many of our favorite British TV shows put on a special created to air during the holidays when people are apt to be watching lots of telly. The special doesn't necessarily have to have anything to do with Christmas but usually does. Some examples from the past include A Blackadder Christmas, Yes Prime Minister, the Vicar of Dibley. Since it's revival in 2005, there's pretty much been a Doctor Who special every year since then. For the last six years there's usually been a Downton Abbey special, sometimes it's festive related. Christmas specials are such a part of the holiday season that the Radio Times (UK TV Guide) puts out a massive double issue featuring everything you can watch while you're eating mince pies and drinking mulled wine.

Mulled Wine

As someone who doesn't drink at all, I had no idea what this one until Mrs Anglotopia was kind enough to inform me. Mulled wine is usually red wine infused with various seasonal mulling spices. It's usually served hot, providing a nice warm drink on a cold winter's day. Port and claret are traditional choices for mulled wine, and are often combined.

Mince Pies

While mincemeat pies no longer have meat in them, they're a delicious Christmas confection enjoyed widely at Christmas. A mince pie is a small British fruit-based mincemeat sweet pie traditionally served during the Christmas season. Its ingredients are traceable to the 13th century, when returning European crusaders brought with them Middle Eastern recipes containing meats, fruits and spices. Now it's a popular treat during Christmas.

Happy Christmas

This one causes a lot of confusion. Merry Christmas is a more traditional Christmas greeting but over the years 'Happy Christmas' is the more common method of wishing holiday merriment in the UK and Ireland. Historically there was 'moral suspicion' around Merry Christmas as it implied boisterousness and drinking. Whereas Happy Christmas is more sedate and sober. The Queen herself wishes her subjects a Happy Christmas in her yearly Christmas Address (see below). As with most things these days, it's a 'to each, his own' type of thing. But most people in the UK say Happy Christmas and it's not because there is some kind of imaginary 'war' on Merry Christmas. In the USA we simply say Merry Christmas instead. Both are perfectly fine.

Father Christmas

This one is easy - Santa Claus, jolly old St Nick. He's the same guy, does the same things, they just call him Father Christmas instead. Visiting Father Christmas isn't as widespread a thing as it is here in the USA but people still do it. You can usually visit him in a Christmas Grotto (often in a Lapland attraction, see below). Harrods has a Christmas Grotto and tickets to see him are released in August and sell out right away!

Lapland

There are usually several of these types of attractions that pop up around the UK during the holiday season. Instead of the North Pole, Father Christmas lives in Lapland (the frozen bits of Finland). To celebrate this people visit Lapland attractions that feature a Grotto (to visit Father Christmas), ice skating, usually a Christmas market, hot drinks, reindeer, etc. It's really an excuse to get in winter gear and go on a day out. And in Great British Tradition, they're usually disappointing.

Chrimbo/Crimble

Chrimbo (sometimes spelled Crimbo) is a British slang word for Christmas that originated in 1928 (though it sounds like something a Chav would say). John Lennon also coined the version Crimble in Beatles' song about Christmas.

Crackers

Crackers are an odd thing. We kind of have them here but they're not common. They're cardboard tubes filled with a paper crown, toy or trinket and usually a joke. They have gunpowder in them and they make a cracking sound when you pull them apart. They're great fun. I personally love the jokes, as lame and awful as they usually are.

Pantomime

No, not the obnoxious street artists in Paris. This is a great British tradition that's the most difficult to explain to non-Brits. A Panto is essentially a play or musical seen at Christmas time. It doesn't have to be Christmas related and is often not. But the plays are ridiculous and usually family friendly. Modern pantomime includes songs, slapstick comedy and dancing, employs gender-crossing actors, and combines topical humour with a story loosely based on a well-known fairy tale. The big shows usually bring in a famous celebrity (often American) to draw in the crowds.

The Queen's Speech

On Christmas day at 3pm, most of the nation stops to hear a special Christmas message from The Queen. It's short and too the point and as a tradition started with the advent of radio. The message is usually a message of good will and understanding and it's the Queen's personal touch to Christmas celebrations that people appreciate the most - it's as if she's speaking right to you. The message is usually recorded in advance and the Queen reflects on the past year and wishes you all a Happy Christmas.

Christmas Pudding

In Britain, Pudding means something completely different than Americans think. A Christmas Pudding is basically a dessert. But it's so much more than a dessert. It has its origins in medieval England, and is sometimes known as plum pudding or just "pud", though this can also refer to other kinds of boiled pudding involving dried fruit. Despite the name "plum pudding," the pudding contains no actual plums due to the pre-Victorian use of the word "plums" as a term for raisins. The pudding is composed of many dried fruits held together by egg and suet, sometimes moistened by treacle or molasses and flavoured with cinnamon, nutmeg, cloves, ginger, and other spices. The pudding is aged for months or even a year; the high alcohol content of the pudding prevents it from spoiling during this time.

German Christmas Markets

This is an odd one for a country that fought two world wars against Germany but one popular German import has been the German Christmas Market. These usually take over the central squares of Britain major cities as local artisans sell often handmade goods with a Christmas themed. They're a good way to pick up a gift or get a nice warm cup of cider or mulled wine.

Christmas Jumper

One tradition that has grown in popularity recently is to have an Ugly Christmas Jumper party in the office. A jumper is a type of pull over sweater and to qualify as a Christmas Jumper is has to have a garish knitted or cross stitched design that you wouldn't be caught dead wearing any other time of the year. It's all for a laugh. Though Grandmother may not appreciate your dislike of her knitted jumpers.

Scottish English Words

Here is a list of common Scottish English words and phrases. This is not meant to be an exhaustive list but an overview of the most commonly used phrases.

Generally, words that are used commonly throughout the rest of Britain have been excluded from the list.

A

Auld - Old.
A-wiz-nae - I was not.
A, ah - I.
Aboot - About.
Aff - Off (off yer heed).
Ah ya bastart - Ouch, that hurt.
Am no - I am not.
Am ur - I am.
Am-ur-nay - I am not.
An empty - The residents who live in the house are not present and people take advantage by having a party in the "empty" house.
Anno - I know.
Arse / erse - Bum.
As-laat - "I was like that"; i.e., I was remarked to say.
Awrite - Alright.
Aye - Yes.

B

Bairn - Baby.
Baltic - Really cold (It's baltic!).
Bampot - An idiot, unhinged person (He is a bampot).
Barras - A short slang term for a place called the Barrowland in the east end of Glasgow.
Bastirt - Bastard, also a term of endearment.
Bawbag - Scrotum, pejorative (That guy's a bawbag).
Bawhair - A recognized unit of measurement.
Baws - Testicles.
Bevvy - Drink.
Bisom - 'Ya wee bisom' which means difficult women, spoilt bratty girl.
Blether - Inane chat.

Bletherskite - To talk rubbish.
Blootered - Drunk.
Boaby - Police. Can also mean penis (She's pure gettin the boaby the night!!).
Boak - To throw up.
Bobee - 6 pence in old money.
Boggin - Smelly, dirty (That's boggin'!).
Bolt - Go away ("wanty bolt!").
Bonglie - Highlanders call tourists 'Bonglies.'
Boot - Ugly woman (Shut it, ya boot!).
Bowfin - Smelly.
Brassic - Skint.
Braw - Beautiful.
Breek - Trousers.
Burd - Girlfriend/Boyfriend.
Burn - Small river (Let's awa' up that burn).

C

Cannae - Can not.
Cannie - Careful (caw cannie be careful).
Chapel - Catholic church ("I am going to chapel on Sunday").
Claes - Clothes.
Clatty bint - Dirty girl.
Cludgie - Toilet.
Crabbit - Crab.
Cummoan - Lets go.
Cushie - Meaning pigeon.

D

Dafty - Silly.
Dancin - Nightclub.
Dead - Usually used with "pure" in front to describe something (That's pure dead brilliant!!!).
Diddy - Did he?
Dinnae - Don't ("Dinnae dae that!").
Dobber - A fool/stupid person. Also means "dickhead" ("Whit ye daein ya dobber?!").
Donner - A walk (comin fur a wee donner doon yonder?).
Doon - Down.
Dreich - Cold as in it's a driech day outside.
Dug - A dog.
Dunderheed - A nice fool.

E

Dejit - Idiot.

F

Dae - From (a ken where yur dae).
Feert - To be scared, afeared (I'm feert of the dark).
Fitbaw - Football.
Fizzog - Face.
Fud - A complete and utter dobber .

G

Gadgie - An old man.
Gan - Go.
Gantin - Smelly/really wanting something.
Geggy - Mouth.
Gingin (pronounced "ging-in") - Disgusting .
Glaikit - A fool.
Glasgow Kiss - A headbutt.
Glesga - Glasgow.
Bobble - Blowjob.
Gomeril - Fool.
Gonnae no dae that - Please do not do that.
Gowpin - Sore body part.
Gran - Grandmother.

Granda - Grandfather.
Guay strangy bairn - Meaning a baby's nappy needs changing!
Gutties - Gym shoes/Trainers.

H

Haar - Fog.
Hackit - Ugly.
Hame - Home "am away hame."
Haud your wheest - Quite.
Hauf ' - A measure of whiskey.
Hawd - Hold, stop "wanty hawd that?"
Hawd yer wheeshd - Stop talking.
Hawn - Hand "watch ma hawn."
Heed/heid - Head "a've got a sare heed."
Honkin - Smelly/dirty.
Hoose - House "it's in ma hoose."
How? - Why?
Howfin/howlin - Smelly.

I

I dinnae ken - Don't know.

J

Jag - An injection.
Jake(y) - A homeless or unkempt person (usually describing an alcoholic).
Jaked - Being in a state of drunkenness (I was jaked last night).
Jessie/jessy - Wimp/big girl's blouse.
Jobby - Poo; plural form "jobbies."

K

Ken - Term for the word 'know.'

L

Lang - Surname.
Lecky - Electricity - often used in reference to bills (she didn't pay her lecky this month).
Liftit - To be arrested by the police.
Loaby - Hallway, lobby, passageway.
Loch - Lake.

Loupin - Cry sore/infested with lice ("My heid is loupin.").

M

Magic - Great/excellent.
Maist - Most.
Maw - Mum (Aye yer maw).
Mawkit/ manky - Very dirty (Your trousers are mawkit!! Ya manky wee bam!!).
Meltit/melted - To be stoned on drugs - (Ah was pure melted man!).
Mibay - Maybe.
Minted - Rich/wealthy ("Look at his motor, he must be minted.).

N

Nae danger - No problem ("Ye want mince and totties fur yur dinner? Nae danger").
Napper - Head.
Naw - No.
Ned - Acronym for 'non-educated delinquent', useless waster, troublemaker.
Neeps – Mashed turnips.

Nip - Kiss a single measure of an alcoholic spirit, often whisky.
Nippin - Stinging.
Numpty - A useless individual/moron.
Nut - 1. Head 2. Or another term used for the word no.

O

Oaf - Off.
Oan yer bike - Go away.
Oan yer trolley - Go away.
Oot - Out.
Outwith - Outside.

P

Pan - Break or disfigure ("pan the windows in").
Peely wally - Pale or pasty.
Pish - Piss.
Pished - Drunk.
Polis - The police.
Pure - Very, totally ("she's pure no right".) used to emphasis something.

Q

Quality - Great/excellent ("That film was quality.").

R

Radge - A fit of rage.
Roamin - Taking a walk.

S

Scheme - Residential area usually council estate.
Scooby - Clue, (no clue).
Scramble - Go away.
Scunner - One who pisses you off.
Scunnered - To be pissed off.
Scunnurt - Fed up (Ah'm pure scunnurt).
Shite - Shit.
Shneck - Kiss.
Shneeb - Smoke.
Shoogle - To take.
Skelp - To smack or hit someone/thing.
Skiddies - Gentleman's undergarments with traces of last nights dinner.
Skuddy - Naked.
Solid - Hard, tough.

Sook - Big softie (ya wee sook).
Squint - Not straight.
Steamin - Drunk.
Stramash - A disturbance, a noisy racket, or a crash
Swallae - To swallow, also means alcohol.

T

Talking oot yer fanny flaps - Lying.
Tan - Smash windows (I'm gonny tan yer windaes).
Tanned - To drink/drunk or to vandalize.
Tap - To borrow money from someone.
Tatties/tatters - Potatoes.
That's a sin - What a shame.
Toaty - Small/tiny.
Tube - An idiot/fool.
Turkish - A piece of poop.
Twally - A person of lesser intellect.

W

Waldies - Wellies.

Wan - One (number or referring to an object or person).
Wean - (pronounced "Wayne") - Child.
Wee – Little/small.
Wee small - A child.
Willy – A man's penis.

Y

Yer erse is oot the windae - You are revealing your bottom.
Yin - One (not the number but referring to a person or object).

West Country English

Here is a sampling of several popular and obsolete words and phrases common in the English West Country. Some of these words may sound familiar from the hit British TV show Doc Martin. We indicate with each word where it's primarily spoken.

Acker (North Somerset, Hampshire, Isle of Wight) - Friend.

Alaska (North Somerset) - I will ask her.

Allernbatch (Devon) - Old sore.

Alright me ansum (Cornwall & Devon) - How are you, my friend?

Alright me babber (Somerset) - Similar to Alright me ansum.

Alright my luvver (just as with the phrase alright mate, when said by a person from the West Country, it has no carnal connotations, it is merely a greeting. Commonly used across the West Country).

Anywhen (Hampshire, Isle of Wight) - At any time.

Appen (Devon) - Perhaps, possibly.

Arable (Devon, Dorset, Somerset, Wiltshire and the Isle of Wight) - (From horrible), often used for a road surface, as in Thic road be arable.

Bad Lot (North Somerset) - E.g. They'm a bad lot, mind.

bauy, bay, bey (Exeter) - Boy.

Beached Whale (Cornwall) - Many meanings, most commonly used to mean a gurt grackle.

Benny (Bristol) - To lose your temper (from a character in Crossroads).

Billy Baker (Yeovil) - Woodlouse.

Bodmin (Cornwall) - Gone crazy.

Boris (Exeter) - Daddy longlegs.

Cheerzen/Cheers'en (Somerset, Bristol) - Thank you (from Cheers, then).

Chinny reckon (North Somerset) - I do not believe you in the slightest (from older West Country English ich ne reckon 'I don't reckon/calculate').

Chine (Isle of Wight) - Steep wooded valley.

Chuggy pig (North Somerset) - Woodlouse.

Chump (North Somerset) - Log (for the fire).

Chuting (North Somerset) - (pronounced shooting) Guttering.

Comical (North Somerset, Isle of Wight) - Peculiar, e.g. 'e were proper comical.

Combe (Devon, Isle of Wight) (pronounced 'coombe') - Steep wooded valley.

Coombe (Devon, North Somerset, Dorset) - Steep wooded valley. Combe/Coombe is the second most common placename element in Devon and is equivalent to the Welsh cwm.

Coupie or Croupie (North Somerset, Dorset, Isle of Wight & Bristol) - Crouch, as in the phrase coupie down.

Crowst (Cornwall) - A picnic lunch, crib.

Cuzzel (Cornwall) - Soft

Daddy granfer (North Somerset) - Woodlouse.

Daps (Bristol, Wiltshire, Dorset, Somerset, Gloucestershire) - Sportshoes (plimsolls or trainers) (also used widely in South Wales).

Diddykai, Diddycoy, Diddy (Isle of Wight, Hampshire) - Gypsy, Traveller.

Dimpsy (Devon) - Describing the state of twilight as in 'it's getting a bit dimpsy.'

Dreckley (Cornwall, Devon, Somerset & Isle of Wight) - Soon, like mañana, but less urgent (from directly once in common English usage for straight away) I be wiv 'ee dreckley.

Drive (Bristol, Somerset & Wiltshire) - Any driver of a taxi or bus. The usual gesture when disembarking from a bus is cheers drive.

Emmet (Cornwall and North Somerset) - Tourist or visitor (derogatory).

Gallybagger (Isle of Wight) - Scarecrow.

Geddon (Crediton, Devon) - Get on, e.g. 'geddon chap!'

Gert Lush (Bristol) - Very good.

Gleanie (North Somerset) - Guinea fowl

Gockey (Cornwall) - Idiot.

Gramersow (Cornwall) - Woodlouse.

Granfergrig (Wiltshire) - Woodlouse.

Grockle (Devon, Dorset, Somerset, Wiltshire and the Isle of Wight) - Tourist, visitor or gypsy (derogatory).

Grockle Shell (Devon, Dorset, Somerset, Wiltshire and the Isle of Wight) - Caravan or motor home (derog).

Gurt (Cornwall, Devon, Somerset, Dorset, Bristol, South Glos and the Isle of Wight) - Big or great, used to express a large size often as extra emphasis That's a gurt big tractor!

Haling (North Somerset) - Coughing.

(H)ang'about (Cornwall, Devon, Somerset, Dorset, Hampshire & the Isle of Wight) - Wait or Pause but often exclaimed when a sudden thought occurs.

Hark at he (Hampshire, Isle of Wight)(pronounced 'ark a' 'ee) - Listen to him.

Headlights (Cornwall) - Light-headedness, giddiness.

Hilts and gilts (North Somerset) - Female and male piglets.

Hinkypunk - Will o' the wisp.

Hucky duck (Somerset, particularly Radstock) - Aqueduct.

Huppenstop (North Somerset) - Raised stone platform where milk churns are left for collection — no longer used but many still exist outside farms.

Ideal (Bristol) - Idea. In Bristol there is a propensity for local speakers to add an l to words ending with a.

Janner (Devon, esp. Plymouth) - A term with various meanings, normally associated with Devon. An old term for someone who makes their living off of the sea. Plymothians are often generally referred to as Janners In Wiltshire, a similar word ' jidder ' is used — possible relation to 'gypsy'.

Janny Reckon (Cornwall and Devon) - Derived from Chinny Reckon and Janner, and is often used in response to a wildly exaggerated fisherman's tale.

Jasper - A Devon word for wasp.

Keendle teening (Cornwall) - Candle lighting.

Kimberlin (Portland) - Someone from Weymouth or further away — not a Portlander.

Madderdo'ee (Cornwall) - Does it matter?

Maid,(devon,exeter) - Girl.

Maggoty (Dorset) - Fanciful.

Mackey (Bristol) - Massive or large, often to benefit.

Mang (Devon) - To mix.

Nipper (Isle of Wight) - A young boy, also a term of endearment between heterosexual men used in the same way as 'mate'.

Now we're farming (Somerset) - Term to describe when something is proceeding nicely or as planned.

Old butt (Gloucestershire, Forest of Dean) - Friend.

Ooh Arr (Devon) - Multiple meanings, including Oh Yes. Popularised by the Wurzels, this phrase has become stereotypical, and is used often to mock speakers of West Country dialects. In the modern day Ooh Ah is commonly used as the correct phrase though mostly avoided due to stereotypes.

Overner (Isle of Wight) - Not from the Island, a mainland person. Extremely common usage.

Parcel of ol' Crams (Devon) - A phrase that sums up and dismisses things that cannot be comprehended or believed.

Piggy widden (Cornwall) - Phrase used to calm babies.

Plimmed, -ing up (North Somerset) - Swollen, swelling.

Poached, -ing up (North Somerset) - Cutting up, of a field, as in the ground's poaching up ,we'll have to bring the cattle indoors for the winter.

Proper job - (Devon, Cornwall, West Dorset, Somerset, Isle of Wight) Something done well

Pummy (Dorset) - Apple pumice from the cider-wring .

Scag (North Somerset) - To tear or catch ("I've scagged me jeans on thacky barbed wire. I've scagged me 'ook up 'round down 'by Swyre 'ed").

Scrage - A scratch or scrape usually on a limb BBC Voices Project.

Slit pigs (North Somerset) - Male piglets that have been castrated.

Smooth (Bristol & Somerset) - To stroke (e.g. cat or dog).

Somewhen (Isle of Wight) - At some time (still very commonly used).

Sprieve (Wiltshire) - Dry after a bath, shower or swim by evaporation.

Spuddler (Devon) - Somebody attempting to stir up trouble. e.g. That's not true, you spuddlin' bugger!

Thic (North Somerset) - That — said knowingly, i.e. to be make dialect deliberately stronger.

Wambling (Dorset) - Wandering, aimless (see A Pair of Blue Eyes by Thomas Hardy)

Wuzzer/wazzin (Exeter) - Was she?/Was he?

Where's it to? - Where is it? (Devon,Dorchester, where's it to? It's in Dorset.)

Young'un - Any young person 'Ow be young un? or where bist goin' youngun?

Zat (Devon) - Soft.

Yorkshire English

Yorkshire English is spoken in the countryside in the North of England and we've put together a short list of words so help you translate. This will be useful when watching a show like All Creatures Great and Small.

'Appen - Perhaps, maybe.
'Ard on - Fast asleep.
'As-ta - Have you.
'At - That.
'Eck - Hell.
'Od - Hold.
'Od on - Wait.
'Oil - Hole, doorway, place.
'Oss - Horse.
'Ouse - 1. Sitting room 2. House.
'Ummer - Heck (NB always used with the and not t').
Aboon - Above.
Addle - Aarn.
Afower - Before.
Agate - To do something.
Agin - Again.
Ah - I.
Alike - Similar.
Allicker - Vinegar.
Allus - Always.
Apiece - Each.
Arran - Spider.
Ax - Ask.
Aye - Yes.

Backend - Autumn.
Backword - To break an agreement or arrangement, cancel.
Bahn - Going/been.
Baht - Without.
Bairn - Child.
Band - String.
Bawl - Cry.
Beck - Stream.
Belong - Come from.
Belt - Hit hard.
Biddy - Louse.
Bide - 1. Wait 2. Like 3. Put up with.
Blowed - Amazed.
Blubberin' - Crying.
Blue murder - Trouble.
Bob - To go ie, just bobbin' out.
Boskin - Stone/wooden/concrete division between tied up cows.
Brass - Money.
Brossen - 1. Full (after a meal) 2. Big headed.
By gum - By God.

Ccack 'anded - 1. Left handed 2. Clumsy.

Capped - Surprised.

Champion - Excellent.

Chimbly/chimly - Chimney.

Chuffed - Proud.

Chump - 1. Gather wood for Bonfire Night 2. Wood.

Chunter - Grumble.

Coil - Coal.

Cop - Catch.

Cumly - Good looking.

Cup - Rose.

Cut - Canal.

Daft - Stupid.

Dahn - Down.

Dee - Die.

Delf - Quarry.

Din - Noise.

Doff - Take off (referring to clothing).

Don - Put on (referring to clothing).

Dooar 'oil - Doorway.

Durns't - Dare not.

Een - Eyes.

Egg on - Encourage.

Et/etten - Ate/eaten.

Fadge - To move with a gait between a jog and a trot.

Fair - Quite.

Feckless - Useless (person).

Fettle - 1. Work 2. Fix 3. Condition.

Flag - Paving stone.

Flaggin' - Tiring.

Flibberty gibbet - Chatterbox.

Flippin' - A mild expletive eg. flippin' 'eck.

Flit - To move house.

Flummox - To confuse.

Fo'ty - Forty.

Forced - Necessarily (used in the negative eg. not forced to be - not necessarily).

Foss - Waterfall.

Fower - Four.

Frame - Shape up (frame yer sen', lad - shape up boy).

Fratch - A fight.

Fresh - 1. New 2. Slightly drunk.

Fust - First.

Gaffer - Boss.

Gallivant - Travel around.

Gallock - Left.

Gallusses - Trouser braces.

Gammy - 1. Injured, lame 2. Bad, off (food).

Ganzy - Pullover.

Gawp - Stare.

Gear - Clothes.

Gerr away - You don't say.

Gill - Half a pint.

Gimmer - 1. Young female sheep 2. An insult (eg. Y'owd gimmer - You silly old person).

Ginnel - Narrow passage between buildings.

Gip - To nearly vomit.

Gob - Mouth.

Gob smacked - Lost for words.

Goit - A small artificial channel carrying water.

Gommeril - Fool.

Goose gogs - Gooseberries.

Gormless - 1. Not intelligent 2. Accident prone.

Grand - Fabulous, very nice, great.

Gumption - Common sense.

Gurt - Big.

I' - In.

Idle - Lazy.

Int' - In the.

Jiggered - Tired.

Jip - Pain.

Kayli - Sherbet.

Keak - To jerk a limb or tilt the head.

Kedge - A glutton.

Kets - Manure spread on a field.

Kist - Chest.

Kit - Milk pail.

Knackers - Testicles.

Lahl - Tittle.

Laik - Play.

Laithe - Barn.

Lame - Painful.

Land - To hit (ie, Ah'll land one on yer - I'll hit you).

Leet - Light.

Lern - Teech.

Let on - Tell.

Lig - Lay (eg, John's ligged out - John's lying down).

Lip - Answer back.

Lowsin' time - Home time.

Lug - 1. Ear 2. Carry.

Mad allik - Reckless.

Maddled - Confused.

Manky - Off (as in food), dirty, smelly.

Mardy - Bad mood.

Mashin' - Brewing a pot of tea.

Mend - Getting healthier.

Mi - Me.

Middlin' - Average.

Mind - Take care (eg, mind yer sen' - take care of yourself).

Missen - Myself, me.

Mistal - Cow shed.

Mother - To bother or harass someone.

Muck - Dirt.

Muck 'oil - Dirty room/house.
Mun - Must.
Na then - 1. Hello 2. Watch it.
Nantle - To fidget or rearrange.
Nay - No.
Neb - Nose.
Nivver - Never.
Nobbut - Only.
Nowt - Nothing.
Offcumden - A person from somewhere else.
Owd - Old.
Ower - Over.
Owt - Anything.
Parkin - A type of ginger cake common at bonfire night.
Parlour - Sitting room.
Pawse - Kick.
Pize - To hit someone.
Quacken - To cure.
Rawk - Thick fog.
Real - Outstanding.
Reckon - Believe.
Reek - Bad smell.
Reet - 1. Right 2. Very.
Reight - Right.
Rive - Tear.
Room - Sitting-room.
Rue - Regret.
Sam up - Gather.

Scunner - North Yorkshire term for an urban youth and usually associated with trouble or petty crime.
Seg - Metal stud for shoes.
Sen - Self.
Sharp - Quick.
Shun - Ignore.
Sickened - Upset.
Side - Clear up.
Sile - Rain heavily.
Sin - Since.
Sitha - See thee here.
Sithee - 'See here'.
Skeg - Glance, look.
Slack - Slow when referring to work/business.
Snap - Packed lunch.
Soft - Weak, cowardly, stupid.
Soz - Sorry.
Spice - Sweets.
Stalled - Bored.
Starved - To be cold.
Suited - Pleased.
Summat - Something.
Sup - Drink, sip.
T' - To.
Tarra - Goodbye.
Teem - Pour heavily as in rain eg. it's teemin' dahn.
Tha'/thou - You.
Think on - Remember.
Thissen - Yourself, you.

Thoil - To be able to justify the expense of a purchase.
Thy - Your.
Thysen - Thyself.
Touched - Simpleton.
Tyke - 1. Yorkshireman 2. Dog.
Umpteen - A lot.
Unheppen - Clumsy.
Us - Me/my or our.
Usen' - Ourselves.
Wahr - Worse.
Waint - Won't or wouldn't.
Wang - Throw.
Watter - Water.
Wed - Married.
Wekken - To wake.
While - Until.
Wi - With.
Wuthering - Blustery, windy.
Y' - You.
Yon - That over there.
Yonder - Over there.
Yorksher - Yorkshire.
Yure - Your.

Scouse English

Scouse English is primarily spoken in the Merseyside area of England and it's closely associated with the city of Liverpool and it's surrounding areas. The Scouse accent is highly distinctive, and has little in common with those used in the neighboring regions of Cheshire and Lancashire. A nickname for some from this area is simply as 'scouser.' Here is a selection of words unique to Scouse English.

'**ad off** - Someone else's poor fortune.

'**ang on a mo'** - please wait a moment.

'**ave off** - a spot of improvised good fortune.

'**ar 'ey** - Oh no!

Arl arse - Cruel.

Arl Fella - Father

Auld baig - Old woman. pron; Owld baig.

Az if - I don't believe that.

Bail - Go Away.

Beaut - An idiot

Better beaut - An extreme idiot

Bevied up - Drunk.

Bevvy - Beer

Bifter - A cigarette or joint

Bizzies, 'de - The Police.

Blag - Lie.

Blaggin' me 'ead - Lying to me.

Blert - A lightweight. Usually from down south.

Blind scouse - Vegetarian version of the scouse national dish.

Bombed out church, de' - St. Luke's.

Boss - Very good.

Butty - Sandwich.

Clobber - Clothes.

Cocky, de' - Night watchman.

Come 'ead - Lets go. Lets do it.

Crocky - Croxteth district. North end.

de' - The.

Deffo - Definitely.

Divvy - A stupid person.

Do one - Go away.

Echo, 'de - Liverpool's evening newspaper that is written and staffed by fools.

Fat Wap - An overweight person.

Gary Ablett's - Ecstasy tablets.

Geggin' in - To join in on something when you aren't invited.

Giz - Give.

Gobshite - Annoying Person or someone who does something stupid.

Is right - I agree.

Is wrong - An argumentative response to is right.

Jarg - counterfeit, fake, poor quality.

Jerk in bed - Birkenhead; a town on the wrong side of the River Mersey.

Jigger - 1. A girocheque. 2. A back alleyway.

Kidder - See la'.

Knock off - Stolen goods.

Knowsley - Officially not Scouseland.

Kopite - LFC (Liverpool Football Club) fan.

La' - Lad.

Lid - See la'.

Made up - Very happy about something.

Manc - A lowly cotton mill worker.

Meff - A smelly, badly dressed person.

N' dat - Something else.

No need - An exclamation of disapproval.

Noggsy - Norris Green district of the city. North end.

North End, de' - North end of the city eg. Noggsy, Crocky, de' Brook, Walton.

On one - To act in a reckless manner.

On top te fuck - A bad situation.

On you - Staking a claim for next go on a spliff.

Ozzy, de' - Hospital.

Paddy's Wigwam - The Catholic Cathedral.

Plazee Scouser - A person who adopts a Scouse accent and mannerisms in attempt to appear cool.

Posh twat - Someone from certain areas of the south end or from down south.

Probe - Legendary Liverpool record label and record store.

Professional Scouser - eg. Jimmy Tarbuck, Cilla Black, Stan Boardman.

Rocket - Beginning and end of the M62 motorway.

royal'ozzy - The Royal Hospital.

Sack it la' - Stop that. Don't do it.

Sayers pastie - Scousers lunch.

Scally - Archetypal Liverpool youth.

Scratch - Signing on the dole.

Shanks - The former legendary Liverpool F.C. manager Bill Shankly.

Skag Head - Heroin addict.

Slotted a boss hatrick - Scored 3 goals.

Soft Lad - Friendly name for a fool.

Sou-ey - Southport, an affluent and small former resort town north of the city. Famous for being robbed blind during English Bank Holidays.

South End, de' - South end of the city eg. Aigy, Speke, Garston see Mud Man, Allerton.

Sozz - Sorry.

Speke - Airport now re-branded as John Lennon International. Also district. South end.

Swerve on it - Not bother with it.

Ta' - Thank you.

Tellin' ye' - Emphasizing agreement.

Texan - A beaut with a high opinion of him/herself.

Tocky - Toxteth district of the city. South end.

Trabs - Sports shoes.

Wabs - Ganja.

Whopper - An idiot.

Woolyback / Wool - A person from Runcorn, Wirral, Wigan, Warrington, Southport etc.

Ye ma - Your mother.

Ye wha? - Pardon.

Yez/Youz - You (plural).

You'll Never Walk Alone - LFC anthem. Show tune popularized by Gerry and his ferry.

25 American Words That Have a Different Meaning in Britain

Every American traveler in Britain has been there - you say something that is completely innocuous back home to a British person and you see wide eyes of shock or worse - you hear a snigger.

Did you just say something rude and not realize it?

It is often said that Britain and America are two countries divided by a common language. There are thousands of differences in American English and plain old English. We thought it would be fun to put together a list of the major words that have a completely different meaning in the UK.

We'll definitely be adding this list to our future travel guidebooks!

1. **First Floor** - In the USA, we say the first floor to mean the ground floor of a building. In the UK, the first floor is the second floor. Confusing? Welcome to the troubles encountered by tourists in the UK.

2. **Jumper** - In the USA a jumper is someone who ends their life by jumping off something. In the UK, a jumper is a type of sweater (usually knitted).

3. **Trainer** - In the USA a trainer is a professional that works with you in a gym. In the UK trainer is the name given to Gym shoes.

4. **Pants** - In the USA, pants are trousers. In the UK, pants are underwear.

5. **Bird** - In the USA, a bird is a bird. In the UK, a bird is a name for a woman (though it's fallen out of fashion as it's rather sexist) but a bird is also just a bird.

6. **Bog** - In both the UK and the USA, a bog is a marshy area of boggy land. In the UK, a bog is also another name for a toilet. Bog roll is toilet paper.

7. **Rubber** - In the USA, a rubber is a condom. In the UK, a rubber is an eraser.

8. **Braces** - In both the UK and USA, braces are devices placed on teeth to straighten them. In the UK, braces also hold up pants (what we call suspenders).

9. **Trolley** - In the USA, a trolley is a public transportation conveyance (most famous in San Francisco). In the UK, a trolley is a shopping cart.

10. **Chips** - In the USA, chips are potato chips (or corn chips). In the UK, chips are what we would call fries but are a chunkier version.

11. **Coach** - In the USA, a coach is someone who manages a sports team. In the UK, a coach is a charter bus.

12. **Fanny Pack** - In the USA a fanny pack is a device worn unfashionably around the waist to store personal effects when traveling. In the UK a fanny is a term for a woman's lady parts. So to call something a fanny pack is a rather offensive term. The Brits call a fanny pack a bum bag (bum is UK speak for butt).

13. **Biscuit** - In the USA, a biscuit is a buttery bread roll. In the UK, a biscuit is a cookie.

14. **Dummy** - In the USA, a dummy is an idiot. In the UK, a dummy is a baby's pacifier.

15. **Flannel** - In the USA, a flannel is a type of button down shirt that's very warm. In the UK, a flannel is a washcloth.

16. **Pissed** - In the USA, to be pissed is to be angry. In the UK, to be pissed is to be fall down drunk.

17. **Fag** - In the USA, fag is a very derogatory term for a homosexual. In the UK, a fag is a cigarette.

18. **Boot** - In both the UK and the USA, a boot is a form of footwear. In the UK, a boot is also the trunk of a car.

19. **Bum** - In the USA, a bum is a homeless person. In the UK, a bum is your butt.

20. **Caravan** - In the USA, a caravan is a type of minivan. In the UK, a caravan is a type of recreational vehicle.

21. **Chaps** - In the USA, chaps are leather pants worn by cowboys or motorcyclists. In the UK, chaps are your male friends.

22. **Chemist** - In the USA, a chemist is a scientist that works with chemicals. In the UK, a chemist is what we would call the pharmacist.

23. **Concession** - In the USA a concession is a place to get snacks in a sporting venue. In the UK, a concession is a discount on a ticket for particular group of people (disabled, student, elderly, etc).

24. **Daddy Long Legs** - In the USA, a daddy long legs is a harmless spider. In the UK, a daddy long legs is also known as the crane fly (but they do have the daddy long legs spider and some refer it to just that).

25. **Post** - In the USA, a post is something in the ground holding something up. In the UK, the post is the mail.

Slang Words and Phrases Coined by Telly

It's often said that William Shakespeare created hundreds of words that we use. This change to the English language continues today with British TV. We thought it would be fun to put together a list of famous words that have been coined by our favorite British TV shows. This list is limited to single or two word phrases.

Smeg

Smeg is a vulgarism or expletive used throughout the sci-fi comedy series of Red Dwarf. Although no specific meaning is ever given, it and its derivatives are regularly used as a derogatory term in place of using actual swear words. The term "Smeghead" is used very commonly throughout as an insult towards characters in the show. Variations of the term include Smeggin' Hell.

TARDIS

The word which is an acronym that means Time and Relative Dimension in Space, TARDIS for short. This is the spaceship piloted by The Doctor, the main character on the long-running science fiction series Doctor Who. It can travel anywhere in time and space and it's bigger on the inside. This has joined the real estate lexicon and it's commonly used to describe a property at 'TARDIS-like' - meaning it looks small on the outside but is bigger on the inside.

Timey-Whimey

A throwaway line from Doctor Who that has become a phrase meant to explain the unexplainable when it comes to time travel (and the show's often non-sensical plots).

Am I bovvered?

From 'The Catherine Tate Show' and it basically means: "I don't care!"

Gone Bodmin

From the hit comedy show Doc Martin -
gone bodmin basically means someone has gone crazy or lost the plot. The show didn't coin the phrase, but it made it popular.

Lovely jubbly

Something that is truly excellent. Wass popularized by the classic British comedy 'Only Fools And Horses', a sitcom watched by over 30m Britons at its peak. Used when a person hear's pleasing news, or gets a stroke of good luck.

Don't panic

This phrase was popularized in World War II comedy Dad's Army but also entered the lexicon from The Hitchhiker's Guide to the Galaxy.

42

This phrase was also made popular by The Hitchhiker's Guide to the Galaxy. What does it mean? Well, everything! The Almighty Answer to the Meaning of Life, the Universe, and Everything. It was calculated by the computer Deep Thought for seven million years and

when asked to build a better computer to discover the Question to the Life, the Universe, and Everything, it built the Earth. Before the Earth could tell
the Question however, it was destroyed by the Vogons to make room for an interstellar highway bypass.

Splunge!

Originating from a Monty Python, splunge is a way of saying that you have no worthy opinion and that an idea could or could not be good. It could also be a quick comeback if you do not have an answer for a question.

Such fun!

Expressed when something extremely amusing occurs. Can also be used to avert or hinder someone from speaking. Frequently used in the British sitcom Miranda.

Spoilers!

While this phrase existed long before it's use on Doctor Who, Doctor Who has made the phrase mainstream. What does it mean? Knowing the end of a story before everyone else. TV Spoilers have become a huge problem in the days of social media. It was used on Doctor Who by River Song to avoid telling the Doctor messy things about his future… and past.

What's occurring?

A phrase coined by the romantic comedy Gavin & Stacey used by the character Nessa whenever she greets someone.

Omnishambles

This one is one of my favorites and was coined on the political comedy show The Thick of It. The phrase was uttered by Malcolm Tucker (brilliantly played by Peter Capaldi) when referring to a situation of total disorder. It has since joined the political lexicon.

British Baby Lingo

With the recent arrival of two royal babies, it's understandable if many of my fellow Americans are confused by some of the terms that British newsreaders are using to describe babies and baby care. So, we thought it would be fun to put together a list of British Baby lingo to help you translate.

- **Pram** - A fancy baby carriage
- **Pushchair** - A step down from a pram for older babies - a stroller.
- **Nappy** - What the British call a diaper.
- **Antenatal** - What the British call pre-natal healthcare.
- **Bairn** - Sometimes how they say baby in Scotland and parts of northern England, such as Newcastle.
- **Little Blighter** - Sometimes used to describe a little boy, slightly derogatory.
- **Dummy** - A pacifier
- **Cot** - A crib
- **Cot death** - SIDS
- **Creche** - Day care or nursery
- **Fairy Cake** - Cupcake
- **Jim-jams** - Pajamas
- **Sick** - Vomit/Throw-up
- **Stabilisers** - Training Wheels on a bike
- **Up the duff** - Impolite way to describe someone as pregnant.
- **Yummy Mummy** - A young, good looking mum (like Mrs. Anglotopia).

- **Wind** - Gas - perfect for describing a gassy baby (like ours unfortunately).
- **Sprog** - Another word for baby.
- **Grizzle** - A fussy baby.
- **Nipper** - A Baby.
- **Moses Basket** - A Bassinet
- **Cotton Wools** - Cotton Balls
- **Baby Grow Suit** - A onesie.
- **Midwife** - Someone who delivers a baby, Doctors are rarely used unless there are complications.

London Street Names

When a city has been around since Roman times, it tends to develop some very unique names for the city streets. Each era of London's history has left its mark on the various streets, avenues, lanes, and ways. Here is a small selection of unique London street and place names and their fascinating histories.

Crooked Usage

The name of this street might be traced back to Anglo-Saxon days, where a usage was a strip of grass between fields. One can assume this particular strip of grass wasn't quite straight.

Jerusalem Passage (see picture above)

Not dedicated to the hymn or a road used by crusaders, Jerusalem Passage was named for an old public house, St. John of Jerusalem, which stood at the northeast corner until 1760.

Knightrider Street

Not to be confused with the classic David Hasselhoff television series (or that crappy modern remake), this street was supposedly the one that knights would take from the Tower of London to Smithfield, where jousts were held.

Fitzroy Square

King Charles II loved the ladies and had several mistresses at court. "Fitz" was a term that meant "illegitimate son of" and "Fitz-roy" is the bastard son of a king. Many of the streets surrounding Fitzroy Square were named after titles created for the many bastard children fathered between Charles and his mistress Barbara Villers, such as Euston, Warren, and Grafton.

Cheapside

"Cheap" doesn't describe the costs of everything along this street. Instead, it's an Old English word meaning "market" (spelled "chepe"). Bread Street, Poultry Street, and Ironmonger Lane were nearby, as well as Stew Lane, which was actually a place for brothels and not food.

Ha Ha Road

A ha-ha is a dry, grassy ditch that serves as a boundary for country estates. The ditch is considered less of an eyesore than a fence while keeping your neighbour's cattle from wandering onto your property. Really harkens back to a time in the city's history when you had to worry about livestock eating your grass.

Little Britain

Actually refers to the Bretons who lived there, an ethnic group originating in Brittany, France. The district was located just north of the London wall. As the rich residents slowly abandoned the neighbourhood, it became the home of many booksellers for a time. The street is mentioned in Charles Dickens' novel, "Great Expectations", as the location of Mr. Jaggers' law office, a place that connects many of the characters.

Great Scotland Yard

Well before the name was associated with law enforcement and the Metropolitan Police, Scotland Yard was an appendage of the royal palace of Whitehall. The buildings there housed the Kings of Scotland and other Scottish dignitaries when they came to visit court. Over time, Whitehall became full of government offices, and eventually the original Metropolitan Police Commissioner had his headquarters at 4 Whitehall Place, the beginning of the street's ties to the Met.

Drury Lane

You know, the one the Muffin Man lives on? Well, it isn't named for him, but for the Drury family who once had an estate here. It gained fame as a street loaded with theatres, the most famous of which is Theatre Royal, which was rebuilt three times following various fires and demolitions.

Cloak Lane

It might make you think of colorful clothing or maybe some kind of ancient fashion or garment district. Well, no such luck. Its name originates from the time when the Romans founded the city and is related to the Cloaca Maxima, one of the world's earliest sewer systems in Rome. You better believe that back when the city was first established, this street didn't smell very good.

French Ordinary Court

What is now a very very short street in London used to house a French "Ordinary" restaurant sometime before the Great Fire. An "ordinary" doesn't mean that the food was regular French fare, but that all the meals were at a fixed price.

Bollocks Terrace

There seems to be no explanation for how this street in Tooting (another funny place) got its name, but if you're familiar with British slang, you'll know that bollocks is another word for testicles, as well as being a statement of untruth (see, "bulls**t").

Shoulder of Mutton Alley

This alleyway found in the area of Tower Hamlets references a popular dish. Mutton is actually sheep's meat, though there are different terms for sheep meat at different ages. A sheep is typically a lamb before the age of one. A hogget refers to a juvenile sheep. Meanwhile, the term "mutton" is reserved for meat from an adult sheep. While this area once may have been known for restaurants, it now serves as a place for young artists.

Shooter's Hill Road

The street and ward of Greenwich it can be found in take their name from being a place for archery practice in the Middle Ages.

Bleeding Heart Yard

No compassion or deadly danger on this street, though an urban legend states that the area was named for the murder of Lady Elizabeth Hatton. Bleeding Heart Yard is a cobblestone courtyard that supposedly drew its name from a tavern of the same name. Charles Dickens references it in Little Dorrit as the home of the Plornish family. Today, the Bleeding Heart Bistro is there serving French cuisine.

Lamb's Conduit Street

Another sheep-related street, this one doesn't actually get its name from the farm animal, but William Lambe, who gave £1,500 to have the road built as a conduit to access water. Lambe also donated 120 pails to poor women so that they could have water for cooking, washing, and bathing.

Pudding Lane

You might think it's got a pretty tasty name, but this street is actually the location where the Great Fire of London kicked off. Its origins are anything but delicious, as the name derives from the entrails and organs that would fall off butchers' carts as they headed from Eastcheap to the River Thames to dump their waste on barges.

Gropecunt Lane

What is now an incredibly rude name for a street actually served a purpose when it first got its name. Even back in the Middle Ages, plenty of towns and cities had a red-light district, including London. The C word, of course, is a pretty offensive word used to describe female body parts. A name like this implied this was a part of town with many houses of ill-repute. Other towns with this name have since changed it to "Gropecount", "Grapecount", "Grape Lane", and more.

Petty France

Not really a name belittling France, it is believed to originate from a group of French Huguenots who settled in the area. Huguenots were French Protestants who fled their native land due to religious persecution. Today, the Ministry of Justice has its headquarters there.

Hanging Sword Alley

Named after a house called the Hanging Sword mentioned in records as having been there in 1574. The character of Jerry Crutchers lived here in Charles Dickens' *A Tale of Two Cities.*

Downing Street

One of the most famous streets in the world, for more than 300 years it has been the home of some of the most powerful leaders in Britain. Its name comes from the man who built it, Sir George Downing, who was politically savvy enough to have worked under both Oliver Cromwell and King Charles II. He built up townhouses along the street in the 1680s and over the centuries, the homes kept being bought up by the government and transformed into official residences and government offices.

Angel, Islington

Angel is just a bit north of Central London and like some of the streets in previous articles, it was named after a pub. The site of the Angel Inn had been in the neighbourhood since the 16th century and today is a historic building that sits on the corner of Islington High Street and Pentonville Road in Islington. The current building was constructed in 1899 and at one point was set to be demolished, but that never happened.

Nunhead Cemetery

During Victorian times, seven cemeteries were built in the outskirts of London to alleviate parish cemetery overcrowding. Dubbed the "Magnificent Seven", Nunhead is considered the least famous among them, but its name is no less unique. The cemetery's name comes from the fact that it's located in Nunhead, which itself comes from a pub named The Nun's Head. As you might expect, the name comes from the actual beheading of a nun that occurred during Henry VIII's dissolution of the monasteries.

The Wick

Located in Richmond, Greater London, this stately home was completed in 1775 by Richard Milne. Though the reason behind the naming of the house is lost to time, its status as a Grade I listed building has attracted several notable residents over the years. Actor Sir John Mills lived there and his wife was inspired by the sound the wind made going around the house to write The Whistle Down the Road. Ronnie Wood of the Rolling Stones lived there for a number of years (with Keith Richards staying in the guest house for a time) before selling it to Pete Townsend of The Who. Pete was less enthused about the sound of the wind and installed new windows because the noise was "driving me crazy."

Postman's Park

Located within the walled section of the city that is the City of London, Postman's Park is one of the largest in that part of London. It was named due to its proximity to the former site of the General Post Office. The interior of the park contains the Memorial to Heroic Self-Sacrifice, dedicated to ordinary people who put their lives on the line to save others, which was built by George Frederic Watts in 1900.

The Hung Drawn and Quartered

Describing itself as "the jewel in the crown of Tower Hill pubs", the name comes from the style of punishment for those persons convicted of treason. As you might expect, the condemned was hung, then disemboweled and beheaded, and finally, his body was chopped into four parts to be placed in areas of prominent display as a warning to any would-be traitors. Today, the pub is practically owned by the brewery Fullers and serves a selection of their ales. It's also close to the Tower of London.

The Cheesegrater

The unofficial name for the skyscraper at 122 Leadenhall Street, the name "Cheesegrater" comes from its distinct wedge shape. Set to be completed this year, it was designed by Richard Rogers and counts several insurance companies amongst its first tenants, including Aon, which is moving its global headquarters from Chicago to London.

Tobacco Dock

Constructed in 1811 on the London Docks, this is a place that does exactly what it says on the tin. It was built originally to house tobacco imported to Britain and now exists as a Grade I listed building. At the north entrance to the building is a seven-foot tall statue of a boy standing in front of a tiger. The story has it that in the late 1800s, Charles Jamrach owned the world's largest exotic pet store near Tobacco Dock and one day, one of his tigers got out. A boy in the street attempted to go up and pet the tiger thinking it was the biggest cat he'd ever seen, only to be carried off by the tiger. Fortunately for the boy (if not the gene pool), Jamrach came out of his shop to chase the tiger down and wrestle the boy away from it (earning him much manliness).

Barking

A town located in East London, the name comes from the Anglo-Saxon word "berecingas", which means either "the settlement of the descendants of Bereca" or "the settlement by the birch trees" (take your pick). Its alleged location as the site of a medieval insane asylum is said to be the origin of the phrase "barking mad".

British Sport

The British sporting world is diverse - the Brits, after all, invented many sports the world loves to play. As you navigate British culture and sport, here is a guide to some of the most common words and phrases you'll encounter.

Association Football - The official name for football or soccer as it is called in the USA.

FA - The official governing body of football, they set the rules and run the leagues.

English Premier League - The Premier League is an English professional league for men's association football clubs. At the top of the English football league system, it is the country's primary football competition. Contested by 20 clubs with a system of relegation for underperforming clubs. There is also a Welsh Premier League and Scottish Premier League, but they are not as internationally popular.

ECB - England Cricket Board - The governing body of Cricket in England and Wales.

The Ashes - The Ashes is a Test cricket series played between England and Australia that is very widely watched. The Ashes are regarded as being held by the team that most recently won the Test series. Held every four years, next will be in 2017-18.

Test Cricket - Test cricket is the longest form of the sport of cricket and is considered its highest standard. Test matches are played between national representative teams with "Test status," as determined by the International Cricket Council (ICC). The two teams of 11 players play a four-innings match, which may last up to five days (or longer in some historical cases). It is generally considered the most complete examination of teams' playing ability and endurance. The name Test stems from the long, grueling match being a "test" of the relative strengths of the two sides.

Six Nations - The Six Nations Championship is an annual international rugby union competition involving six European sides: England, France, Ireland, Italy, Scotland, and Wales.

Rugby Union - Rugby union, known in some parts of the world simply as rugby, is a contact team sport which originated in England in the first half of the 19th century. One of the two codes of rugby football, it is based on running with the ball in hand. In its most common form, a game is between two teams of 15 players using an oval-shaped ball on a rectangular field with H-shaped goalposts on each try line.

Rugby League - Rugby league football, usually called rugby league, is a full contact sport played by two teams of thirteen players on a rectangular field. One of the two codes of rugby football, it originated in England in 1895 as a split from the Rugby Football Union over the issue of payments to players. Its rules gradually changed with the aim of producing a faster, more entertaining game for spectators. In rugby league, points are scored by carrying the ball and touching it to the ground beyond the opposing team's goal line; this is called a try and is the primary method of scoring

FIFA - The official international body that manages the rules and regulations of Football. They also set up the framework for each country's national team.

UEFA - The Union of European Football Associations is the administrative body for association football in Europe, although several member states are primarily or entirely located in Asia. It is one of six continental confederations of world football's governing body FIFA. **UEFA** consists of 55 national association members.

World Cup - International Competition held every four years where the top national teams compete for the world championship. Run by FIFA. Next will be in 2018.

UEFA European Championship (Euro Cup) - Championship competition featuring national teams from European countries only, held every four years and managed by UEFA. Usually held two years after/before the next World Cup. Next will begin 2020.

Rugby World Cup - The Rugby World Cup is a men's rugby union tournament contested every four years between the top international teams. The tournament was first held in 1987 when the tournament was co-hosted by New Zealand and Australia. New Zealand are the current champions, having defeated Australia in the final of the 2015 tournament in England.

Wimbledon - General term for The Championships, Wimbledon, the oldest tennis tournament held in the world every June.

All England Club - The All England Lawn Tennis and Croquet Club, also known as the All-England Club, based at Church Road, Wimbledon, London, England, is a private members' club. It is best known as the venue for the Wimbledon Championships, the only Grand Slam tennis event still held on grass.

Snooker - Snooker is a cue sport which originated in India in the latter half of the 19th century. It is played on a table covered with a green cloth, or baize, with pockets at each of the four corners and in the middle of each side cushion. Using a cue and 22 colored balls, players must strike the white ball (or "cue ball") to pot the remaining balls in the correct sequence, accumulating points for each pot.

The Boat Race - The Boat Race is an annual rowing race between the Oxford University Boat Club and the Cambridge University Boat Club, rowed between men's open-weight eights on the River Thames in London, England. It is also known as the University Boat Race and the Oxford and Cambridge Boat Race.

Names of Britain

There are so many names for the United Kingdom that it can be hard to keep them straight. Some were used interchangeably as if they mean the same thing. Some are used incorrectly. Oftentimes people are mistaken when they refer to something in Scotland as being in England or that the word 'English' means the same thing as 'British.'

So, we thought it would be fun to put together a list of words and explanations for some of the places and peoples in the United Kingdom.

UK - The official name is the United Kingdom of Great Britain and Northern Ireland, which consists of England, Wales, Scotland, and Northern Ireland.

(Great) Britain - The island of Great Britain itself but often used when talking about the United Kingdom. Does not include Northern Ireland.

British - A term usually used to mean anyone from the United Kingdom though this may annoy the Northern Irish. It is also not advisable to call a Scotsmen British. While they are technically British, they are Scottish first. Someone like Andy Murray is Scottish until he's winning at Wimbledon at which point he becomes British.

Britannia - An outdated Latin term for the island of Great Britain that was coined by the Romans. They also founded Londinium, the city that became London. Britannia is also the female symbol of the UK - the shield maiden used on older currency. Britannia was also a symbol of British Imperialism.

Briton - Essentially a citizen of the United Kingdom, the Isle of Man, the Channel Islands, or of one of the British Overseas Territories. The shortened version is 'Brit' which is commonly used by Americans to refer to the British. There are many who don't like usage of that term.

The British Isles - The Geographic name for the islands that make of Great Britain and Ireland, though it's falling out of use because the Irish don't like being called British for good reason.

Hibernia - Classical Latin name for Ireland.

Éire - Irish Gaelic for Ireland

Albion - Another outdated term for the island of Great Britain. This is the oldest known name of the island and comes from Ancient Greek.

Caledonia - The Latin name given to the northern part of Britannia which is now called Scotland.

Cymru - The Welsh language name for Wales.

Ulster - The northern, UK part of the island of Ireland (the independent Republic of Ireland is the bottom part).

England - The largest country in the United Kingdom, where most people live in the UK. South of Scotland and East of Wales.

English - 1. The language spoken by the British (but as in Scotland and Wales, not the only language). 2. The people who live in England. Someone from Scotland is not English. Someone from Wales is not English. Only someone from England is English

Blighty - An older term for 'Britain' that evokes misty-eyed golden images of Britain. 'Dear Old Blighty.' Originated in India, but adopted its present day meaning during the Boer War.

Rosbif - A derogatory French term used by the French to describe the British. Because the British love Roast Beef (or at least that's what the French think).

Sassenach - Term used by the Scottish and other Celts to describe the English.

Team GB - The official Olympics team for Scotland, England, Wales and Northern Ireland. Some people believe the name discriminates against the Northern Irish.

Grande Bretagne - French for Great Britain.

Angleterre - French for England.

Grossbritannien - German for Great Britain

Gran Bretagna - Italian for Great Britain

Names of London

LONDON – the very name strikes such a cord with people who love that fair city. It conjures up an image of beautiful buildings, long history, the Thames, black taxis, red buses, red phone boxes, charming locals, and so much more.

London has been known by several names throughout its history and it also has different names all over the world based on the language spoken.

Here's a fun list of a few.

Londinium – This was the original Roman name for the city they founded on the banks of the Thames and the root of all the future iterations. It varied based on language and translation – here are some examples: c. 115; Londinion c. 150; Londinio, Lundinio 4th century; Lundinium late 4th century; and Londini early 2nd century and c. 105.

Lundenwic – The port on the Thames founded by the Anglo-Saxons in the 7th or 8th century about a mile away from the original Londinium settlement. It means literally 'London settlement or trading town.'

Londontown – A colloquial and affectionate nickname for London. Not quite accurate as London has never been a town – it's always been a city from its founding. The phrase was made famous by the song *A Nightingale Sang in Berkley Square* and later in an album called *London Town* by Sir Paul McCartney.

Londres – This is the the French, Catalan, Portuguese, Spanish, and Filipino language name for London. The 'r' is silent and is pronounced as you would in Italian (see below).

Londra – Italian name for London.

The Big Smoke – London was given this label in the 19th century due to its choking smog and pollution caused by coal burning fires. It's a name that stuck as another name for London. It's also been known as The Old Smoke. London's legendary fog became a relic of history thanks to air pollution laws in the 1950s and 1960s.

City of London – The Square Mile – This is the original settlement that forms the core of London. It's about 1 square mile in size on the banks of the Thames and it has its own government structure separate from the rest of London. The outline of the City is still made up of the outlines of the original Roman Wall (and you can still see bits of it in random places around the City).

Greater London Authority – The current overall government for all the various boroughs that make up London. It has a mayor (currently Sadiq Khan) and an elected assembly with 25 members. It's only been around since the year 2000 when it was created by the Labour government. It is made up of the 32 boroughs in the historical London area along with the City of London (which has its own government).

London County Council – The former authority that governed London but it was abolished by Margaret Thatcher in 1986 (it was political, she hated its leader Ken Livingstone – later London's first elected mayor). Its grand building is now home to some of London's most popular tourist attractions such as the London Aquarium and the London Dungeon.

Metroland – An informal name for a suburban area northwest of London, England, served by the Metropolitan Line on the London Underground. It now has come to represent the golden age idea of London suburban life in the pre-World War II era as London spread out into suburbia via the Tube and other rail lines.

LHR – The airport abbreviation for London Heathrow airport.

LGW – The airport abbreviation for London Gatwick airport.

London City – The small airport located in the Docklands that has short haul flights to the rest of Europe.

LDN – The new shortened version of London often used in marketing but also used by people sending text messages.

10 British Villages with Unique Names

It's not just streets and roads in London that have unique names, many of Britain's villages have them as well. As this article shows, there are plenty of unique names in the whole of England, Scotland, Wales, and Northern Ireland. Of course, what you think their names might mean and where they originate can be very very different.

Beer

Located in Devon, the Village of Beer is not named after the alcoholic beverage. Instead, its name comes from the Anglo-Saxon word "bearu", which meant grove, like the one that surrounded the village long ago. Located along the southern coast, it had a pretty good fishing industry once upon a time, but also was a point for smugglers to bring their goods into the country.

Crackpot

This village in North Yorkshire derives its name from the Old English word "kraka" (or crow) and the Viking word "pot" (meaning a deep hole, in this case, a rift in limestone). Crackpot Cave has a pretty impressive geological feature, a column made from an intersecting stalactite and stalagmite.

Lost

More a hamlet than a village, only about two dozen people live in Lost. The name comes from the Scots Gaelic word for inn, taigh ósda, with the village's name being Lósda in Gaelic. The Aberdeenshire Council wanted to change the name to "Lost Farm" after a number of understandable thefts of the village sign, but the some two-dozen people who lived there resisted and eventually the Council let them keep the name.

Three Cocks

Get your mind out of the gutter, lad, or you'll be doing lines for the rest of term! The Welsh name for this village located in Powys is Aberllynfi. The English name is a relatively recent addition, taken from the former Three Cocks railway junction (now a garden centre), which itself was named for the Three Cocks Inn (which is still there), which *itself* was named for the heraldry of the Williams family who were local landowners.

Muff

That's it, lad, to the headmaster's office with you! Found in County Donegal of Northern Ireland, it sits right on the border with the Republic of Ireland. Its Irish name is Magh and plays host to the Muff Festival every year, including competitions, street parties, and music performances. It is also home to the "swear-to-God-I'm-not-making-this-up" Muff Diving Club. The club offers discounts for its members at Malin Head Wrecks in County Donegal, a place for divers to check out shipwrecks from WWI and WWII.

Ugley

This hamlet in Essex has no alibi (think about that joke for a second). The first documentation of its name is in 1041 as "Uggele" and later in the Domesday Book as "Ugghelea". Its name may mean "woodland clearing of a man named Ugga". Ugley has at least two Grade II listed buildings that are anything but ugly.

Pratts Bottom

Found in Kent, Pratt comes from the Latin word "partum" meaning "meadow", though another sources suggests that it means "valley of a family called Pratt". The village is part of Greater London and the Borough of Bromley.

Shitterton

I do apologize for all this bottom humour (not really). Another hamlet, this one located in Dorset, has a name that literally meant "town on the stream of a sewer". A survey back in 2012 named this the most unfortunate place name in Britain. As with Lost, town residents have had to suffer numerous thefts of their sign and they eventually replaced it with a stone one that's much harder to lift.

Brokenwind

Don't breathe in too deeply in this Scottish hamlet. The name was spelt "Broken Wynd" in the 19th Century and actually referenced a narrow path that winds up between two larger roads.

Bitchfield

Not a place where you can make complaints, this village in Lincolnshire first appeared in the Domesday Book as Billesfelt. Apparently, the best thing to see there is the local parish church, which provides practically unaltered Norman and Perpendicular Gothic architecture.

Funny British Place Names

Britain is a land of geographic linguistic variety, with some names going back thousands of years, this leads to amusement when a name from long ago means something completely different in the modern era. With that said, here's our list of amusing places names located throughout the United Kingdom.

London

- Back Passage, London
- Mincing Lane, London
- Mudchute, London
- Percy Passage, London
- Swallow Passage, London
- Trump Street, London
- Cumming Street, London
- Cockfoster, London
- Dick Turpin Lane, London
- Cock Hill, London
- Titley Close, London
- Cockbush Avenue, London

England

- Acock's Green, Worcestershire
- Babes Well, Durham
- Bachelors Bump, Essex
- Backside Lane, Oxfordshire
- Balls Green, Kent, England
- Balls Cross, WestSussex
- Bareleg Hill, Staffordshire
- Barking, Essex
- Beaver Close, Surrey
- Bedlam Bottom, Hampshire
- Beef Lane, Oxfordshire
- Beer, Devon

- Beggars Bush, Sussex passed her prime
- Bell End near Lickey End
- Bishops Itchington, Staffs
- Bitchfield, Lincolnshire
- Boggy Bottom, Abbots Langley, Herts
- Booty Lane, NorthYorkshire
- Bottoms Fold, Lancashire
- Broadbottom, Cheshire
- Brown Willy, Cornwall
- Bushygap, Northumberland
- Catholes, Cumbria
- Catsgore, Somerset
- Charles Bottom, Devon
- Clap Hill, village in Kent
- Clay Bottom, Bristol
- Cock Alley, Calow
- Cock Bridge, Hope, Derbyshire
- Cock Green, nr Braintree
- Cock Lane, Tutts Clump, Berkshire
- Cock Law, Northumberland
- Cock and Bell Lane, Suffolk
- Cockermouth, Cumbria
- Cockernhoe, nr Luton
- Cocking, Midhurst, West Sussex
- Cockintake, Staffordshire
- Cockpit Hill, Derbyshire
- Cockplay, Northumberland
- Cocks, Cornwall
- Cockshoot Close, Oxfordshire
- Cockshot, Northumberland
- Cockshutt Wood, Sheffield
- Cockup Lake District, Cumbria. UK
- Coldwind, Cornwall
- Crackington Haven, Cornwall, UK
- Crackpot, North Yorkshire
- Crapstone, Devon
- Crotch Crescent, Oxford
- Deans Bottom, Kent
- Devil's Lapful, Northumberland

- Dicks Mount, Suffolk
- Drinkstone, Suffolk
- Faggot, Northumberland
- Fanny Barks, Durham
- Fanny Avenue, Derbyshire
- Fanny Hands Lane, Lincolnshire
- Feltham Close, Hampshire
- Feltwell, Norfolk
- Fingringhoe, Essex
- Flesh Shank, Northumberland
- Friars Entry, Oxfordshire
- Fruitfall Cove, Cornwall
- Fudgepack upon Humber, Humberside
- Gay Street, Sussex
- Gays Hill, Cornwall
- Giggleswick, Staincliffe, Nth. Yorkshire
- Golden Balls, Oxfordshire,
- Gravelly Bottom Road, nr Langley Heath, Kent
- Great Cockup & Little Cockup, hills in The Lake District
- Great Horwood, Bucks
- Great Tosson, Northumberland
- Grope Lane, Shropshire
- Hampton Gay, Oxfordshire
- Happy Bottom, Dorset
- Helstone, Cornwall
- Hole Bottom, Yorkshire
- Hole of Horcum, North Yorkshire
- Holly Bush, Ledbury, Herefordshire
- Honey Knob Hill, Wiltshire
- Honeypot Lane, Leicestershire
- Hooker Road, Norwich
- Horncastle, Linconshire
- Horneyman, Kent
- Hornyold Road, Malvern Wells, UK
- Horwood, Devon
- Jeffries Passage, Surrey
- Jolly's Bottom, Cornwall
- Juggs Close, EastSussex

- Knockerdown, Derbyshire
- Letch Lane, Bourton-on-the-Water, The Cotswolds
- Lickar Moor, Northumberland
- Lickers Lane, Merseyside
- Lickey End, Worcestershire
- Lickfold, West Sussex
- Little Horwood, Bucks
- Little Bushey Lane, Hertfordshire
- Long Lover Lane, Halifax
- Lower Swell, Gloucestershire
- Menlove Avenue, Liverpool
- Minge Lane, Worcestershire
- Moisty Lane, Staffordshire
- Nether Wallop, Hampshire
- Nob End, South Lancashire
- Nork Rise, Surrey
- North Piddle, Worcestershire
- Ogle Close, Merseyside
- Old Sodbury, Gloucestershire
- Old Sodom Lane, Wiltshire
- Over Peover, Cheshire
- Pant, Shropshire
- Penistone, Sth Yorkshire
- Piddle River, Dorset
- Pork Lane, Essex
- Pratt's Bottom, Kent
- Prickwillow, Cambridgeshire
- Pump Alley, Middlesex
- Ram Alley, Wiltshire
- Ramsbottom, Lancs
- Rimswell, East Riding of Yorkshire
- Sandy Balls, Hampshire
- Scratchy Bottom, Dorset
- Shaggs, Dorset
- Shingaycum Wendy, Buckinghamshire
- Shitlingthorpe, Yorkshire
- Shitterton, Dorset
- Six Mile Bottom, Cambridge
- Slackbottom, Yorkshire
- Slag Lane, Merseyside
- Slip End, Beds

- Slippery Lane, Staffordshire
- Snatchup, Hertfordshire
- Spanker Lane, Derbyshire.
- Spital-in-the-Street, Lincolnshire
- Splatt, Cornwall
- Staines, Surrey
- Stow cum Quy, Cambridgeshire
- Swell, Somerset
- The Blind Fiddler, Cornwall
- The Bush, Buckinghamshire
- The Furry, Cornwall
- The Knob, Oxfordshire
- Thong, Kent
- Tinkerbush Lane, Oxfordshire
- Titcomb, near Inkpen, Berkshire
- Titlington Mount, Northumberland
- Titty Hill, Sussex
- Titty Ho, Northamptonshire
- Tosside, Lancashire
- Turkey Cock Lane, Colchester, Essex
- Ugley, Essex
- Upper Bleeding, Sussex
- Upper Chute, Hampshire
- Upper Dicker & Lower Dicker, East Sussex
- Upperthong, West Riding, Yorkshire
- Wash Dyke, Norfolk
- Weedon Lois, Northampton
- Weedon, in the Parish of Hardwick, Buckinghamshire
- Weeford, Staffordshire
- Wet Rain, Yorkshire
- Wetwang, East Yorkshire
- WhamBottomLane, Lancashire
- Wideopen, Newcastle
- Willey, Warwickshire
- Winkle Street, Southampton
- Wormegay, Norfolk

Scotland

- Ardfork, Aberdeenshire
- Ardgay, Ross & Cromarty
- Assloss, Ayrshire
- Backside, Aberdeenshire
- Backside, Banffshire
- Ballownie, Angus
- Blackdikes, Angus
- Bladda, Paisley
- Forest Dyke Road, Lanarkshire
- Boghead, Ayrshire
- Boysack, Angus
- Brokenwind, Aberdeenshire
- Butt of Lewis, Hebrides
- Cock of Arran, Isle of Arran
- Cumloden Court, Dumfries and Galloway
- Dick Court, Lanarkshire
- East Breast, Inverclyde
- Fannyfield, Ross and Cromarty
- Fattiehead, Banffshire
- Hillo'ManyStanes
- Inchbare, Angus
- Inchinnan Drive, Renfrewshire
- Inchmore, Aberdeenshire
- Merkins Avenue, West Dumbartonshire
- Stripeside, Banffshire
- Tarty, Aberdeenshire
- The Bastard, a mountain in Scotland
- Twatt, Orkney

Wales

- Bullyhole Bottom, Monmouthshire
- Cat's Ash, Monmouthshire
- Pant-y-Felin Road
- Penisarwaen, village in Gwynedd
- Sodom, Flintshire
- Splott, Cardiff
- St.Mellons, Cardiff
- Stop-and-Call, Pembrokeshire
- Tarts Hill, Flintshire
- Three Cocks, Breconshire

Phrases We Owe To Shakespeare

Shakespeare is without a doubt a man that had the most effect on the English language and the way that we use it today. In an effort to find out just how much he has influenced how we speak today, I thought it would be fun to put together a list of phrases that can be attributed to him and his plays. These are from multiple sources, and I've culled them together into one massive list.

Enjoy!

- A countenance more in sorrow than in anger
- A Daniel come to judgment
- A dish fit for the gods
- A fool's paradise
- A foregone conclusion
- A horse! A horse! My kingdom for a horse!
- A ministering angel shall my sister be
- A plague on both your houses
- A rose by any other name would smell as sweet
- A sea change
- A sorry sight
- A tower of strength
- Age cannot wither her, nor custom stale her infinite variety
- Alas, poor Yorick! I knew him, Horatio
- All corners of the world
- All one to me

- All that glitters is not gold / All that glisters is not gold
- All the world's a stage, and all the men and women merely players
- All's well that ends well
- An eye-sore
- An ill-favoured thing sir, but mine own
- And shining morning face, creeping like a snail unwillingly to school
- And thereby hangs a tale
- As cold as any stone
- As dead as a doornail
- As flies to wanton boys are we to the gods
- As good luck would have it
- As merry as the day is long
- As white as driven snow
- At one fell swoop
- Ay, there's the rub
- Bag and baggage
- Bated breath
- Beast with two backs
- Beware the ides of March
- Blow, winds, and crack your cheeks
- Breathe one's last
- Brevity is the soul of wit
- Budge an inch
- Cold comfort
- Come full circle
- Come the three corners of the world in arms
- Come what may
- Comparisons are odorous
- Conscience does make cowards of us all
- Cowards die many times before their deaths
- Crack of doom
- Cry havoc and let slip the dogs of war
- Dash to pieces
- Dead as a doornail
- Death by inches
- Discretion is the better part of valour

- Dish fit for the gods
- Dog will have its day
- Double, double toil and trouble, fire burn, and cauldron bubble
- Eaten me out of house and home
- Elbow room
- Et tu, Brute
- Even at the turning of the tide
- Every inch a king
- Exceedingly well read
- Eye of newt and toe of frog, wool of bat and tongue of dog
- Fair play
- Fancy free
- Fatal vision
- Fie, foh, and fum, I smell the blood of a British man
- Fight fire with fire
- For ever and a day
- Foul play
- Frailty, thy name is woman
- Friends, Romans, countrymen, lend me your ears
- Full of sound and fury
- Get thee to a nunnery
- Give the devil his due
- Good men and true
- Good night, ladies
- Good riddance
- Green eyed monster
- Hark, hark! the lark at heaven's gate sings
- He will give the Devil his due
- Heart's content
- High time
- His beard was as white as snow
- Hoist by your own petard
- Hold a candle to
- Hot-blooded
- Household words
- How sharper than a serpent's tooth it is to have a thankless child
- I bear a charmed life
- I have not slept one wink
- I see you stand like greyhounds in the slips

- I will wear my heart upon my sleeve
- If music be the food of love, play on
- In a pickle
- In my heart of hearts
- In my mind's eye
- In stitches
- In the twinkling of an eye
- Into thin air
- Is this a dagger which I see before me?
- It beggar'd all description
- It is meat and drink to me
- It smells to heaven
- It was Greek to me
- It's a wise father that knows his own child
- Kill ... with kindness
- Knock, knock! Who's there?
- Laughing-stock
- Lay it on with a trowel
- Lean and hungry look
- Let slip the dogs of war
- Lie low
- Like the Dickens
- Lord, what fools these mortals be!
- Love is blind
- Make your hair stand on end
- Men's evil manners live in brass; their virtues we write in water
- Milk of human kindness
- Misery acquaints a man with strange bedfellows
- More fool you
- More honoured in the breach than in the observance
- More in sorrow than in anger
- More sinned against than sinning
- Much Ado about Nothing
- Mum's the word
- Murder most foul
- My own flesh and blood
- My salad days

- Neither a borrower nor a lender be
- Night owl
- No more cakes and ale?
- Not a mouse stirring
- Now is the winter of our discontent
- O Romeo, Romeo! wherefore art thou Romeo
- O, Brave new world
- Off with his head
- Oh, that way madness lies
- Once more unto the breach, dear friends, once more
- One fell swoop
- One that loved not wisely, but too well
- Out of the jaws of death
- Out, damned spot!
- Parting is such sweet sorrow
- Play fast and loose
- Pomp and Circumstance
- Pound of flesh
- Primrose path
- Rhyme nor reason
- Sans teeth, sans eyes, sans taste, sans everything
- Screw your courage to the sticking place
- Send him packing
- Set your teeth on edge
- Shall I compare thee to a summer's day?
- Sharper than a serpent's tooth
- Short and the long of It
- Short shrift
- Shuffle off this mortal coil
- Smooth runs the water where the brook is deep
- Some are born great, some achieve greatness, and some have greatness thrust upon 'em
- Something in the wind
- Something is rotten in the state of Denmark
- Sorry sight

- Spotless reputation
- Star crossed lovers
- Stiffen the sinews
- Stony hearted
- Stood on ceremonies
- Strange bedfellows
- Such stuff as dreams are made on
- Sweets to the sweet
- The be-all and the end-all
- The better part of valour is discretion
- The course of true love never did run smooth
- The crack of doom
- The devil can cite Scripture for his purpose
- The Devil incarnate
- The first thing we do, let's kill all the lawyers
- The game is afoot
- The game is up
- The lady doth protest too much, methinks
- The naked truth
- The play's the thing
- The quality of mercy is not strained
- The Queen's English
- The slings and arrows of outrageous fortune
- The smallest worm will turn, being trodden on
- The working day world
- The world's mine oyster
- There is a tide in the affairs of men
- There's method in my madness
- Thereby hangs a tale
- This is the short and the long of it
- This is very midsummer madness
- This precious stone set in the silver sea, this sceptered isle

- This was the noblest Roman of them all
- Though this be madness, yet there is method in it
- Throw cold water on it
- Thus far into the bowels of the land
- Tis neither here nor there
- To be or not to be, that is the question
- To gild refined gold, to paint the lily
- To make a virtue of necessity
- To sleep: perchance to dream
- To thine own self be true
- Too much of a good thing
- Truth will out
- Under the greenwood tree
- Uneasy lies the head that wears a crown
- Unkindest cut of all
- Up in arms
- Vanish into thin air
- We are such stuff as dreams are made on
- We few, we happy few, we band of brothers
- We have seen better days
- Wear my heart on my sleeve
- What a piece of work is a man
- What the dickens
- What's done is done
- What's in a name?
- What's in a name? That which we call a rose by any other name would smell as sweet
- When sorrows come, they come not single spies, but in battalions
- Where the bee sucks, there suck I
- While you live, tell truth and shame the Devil!
- Who wooed in haste, and means to wed at leisure
- Wild goose chase
- Woe is me

Australian English

Here's a quick guide to Australian English slang words. You'll definitely see the influences of American and British English on Australian Slang but you'll also see words that mean something completely different than you think. It's a fun list!

A

Ace - Excellent, very good.

Aggro – Aggressive or aggravation.

Apples, she's - Everything is all right; often modified with will as in she'll be apples.

Arsey - Someone showing daring, audacity, and/or cheekiness.

Not being arsed - Lack of interest, as in "I couldn't be arsed to do it". Also British English.

Arvo - Short for afternoon; in use since the 1950s.

As if - Exclamatory rejection. "As if they're real tears!" or "The case was dismissed? As if."

Aussie salute - Brushing away flies with the hand.

B

B & S - In full Bachelors' and Spinsters' Ball - a party/function held for young single people.

Bag - (v) To denigrate; (n) An ugly woman; both senses in use since the 1960s.

Bags - To reserve, as in "(I) Bags the last frosty fruit (ice block)" or "Can someone do the dishes?" "Bags not!"

Bail (somebody) up - To corner somebody.

Bang - Sexual intercourse.

Barkers eggs - Dog poo.

Beaut - Great, fantastic, terrific.

Beauty - Exclamation showing approval, often spelt as bewdy.

Beef - To have a problem with someone.

Bickie - Biscuit. Sometimes also used as a word for a cigarette lighter, after the manufacturer Bic.

Big bickies - Lots of money.

Big-note oneself - To brag or boast.

Bizzo – Business.

Biff or biffo - A brawl or fist fight.

Bitser - Dog of mixed parentage, mongrel.

Blow - A rest, especially after physical work.

Bloody - Very (bloody hard yakka).

Bloody oath - That's certainly true; used as an affirmative to a statement.

Blue - A fight, brawl or heated argument or an embarrassing mistake.

Bluey - Formerly, a bundle of belongings wrapped in a blanket carried by swagmen.

Bludge - To shirk, be idle, or waste time either doing nothing or something inappropriate.

Bodgy - Of inferior quality.

Bog in - Commence eating, to attack a meal with enthusiasm.

Bog standard - Basic, unadorned, without accessories .

Bomb - An old mechanically unsound car. "That car is a bomb."

Bonzer - Great, ripper.

Boogie board - A hybrid, half-sized surf board.

Boong - A term lately considered highly derogatory, used for Australian Aboriginals.

Bottler - Something excellent.

Brumbie - Wild (as in undomesticated) horse.

Buck's night - Stag party, male gathering the night before the wedding.

Buggered (1) - Tired. "I'm feeling buggered."

Buggered (2) - Broken, not in working order. "That hose is buggered."

Buggered (3) - In trouble, or caught out. "I was caught speeding, I'm buggered!"

Built like a brick shithouse - Being strongly built.

Bundy - A nickname for a brand of rum (Bundaberg Rum).

Bung - Originally a stopper in a cask; a synonym for "put" or "place"; as in "bung it in the oven" or not working, broken, impaired, injured or infected.

Bung it on - To put on a show of pretence.

Bush - Woodland, generally called bushland, rural Australia.

Bush bashing - To force a path through the bush either by bushwalking or driving a 4WD (SUV) or the like.

Bush bash - A long competitive running or motorcar race through the bush.

Bushfire - Wild forest fire.

Bushie - A person living in remote rural areas,

Bush oyster - A gob of expelled nasal mucus.

Bush telly – Campfire.

Bushman's hanky - Emitting nasal mucus by placing one index finger on the outside of the nose (thus blocking one nostril) and blowing.

Bushwalking - Hiking in the bush.

Buttsucker - Someone who smokes cigarettes.

C

Cackleberry - Egg

Cactus - Dead, non-functional, not functioning.

Cark it - To die or to cease functioning.

Carn - Assimilation of "come on!" or "Go on!"; usually used to either goad someone.

Cat's pyjamas or cat's whiskers - Something great or perfectly suited, as in.

Cattle duffer - A cattle rustler.

Chook - A chicken.

Chrissie - Christmas

Chuck a sickie - Take the day off sick from work when you're perfectly healthy.

Chunder - Vomit. "I had a chunder."

Clayton's - Fake, substitute, not the real thing, ersatz.

Clucky - Feeling broody or maternal.

Cockie – Farmer; also short for 'cockatoo', an Australian bird.

Come a gutser - Make a bad mistake, have an accident.

Compo - Workers' compensation pay.

Cossie, cozzie - Swimming costume, bathers.

Cranky - In a bad mood, angry.

Crikey - An exclamation of surprise.

Crook - Angry, in the phrase "go crook at", sick or unwell, unfair.

Crunk - To get drunk.

Culosis - A resigned expression of frustration.

Cut - angry or upset.

D

Dag - An unfashionable or uncool person, equivalent to "geek" or "dork".

Daggy - Unfashionable, uncool, "nerdy", "dorky."

Darl - Term of endearment usually used for one's spouse: shortening of darling.

Dead set - (adj) Certain; indisputable; (adv) Completely "You're dead set right about that."

Deadly – Excellent.

Devo - Devastated or deviant.

Der - That's obvious, duh.

Derro - A term for idiot , someone who is stupid, or has done something ridiculous.

Deso - The designated driver on a night out.

Dekko - A look, to inspect something.

Dink - To give somebody a lift on the back of a bicycle.

Dinger – Condom.

Dinkum - Honest, genuine, real. Often preceded by the word "fair", as in "fair dinkum."

Dinky-di - The real thing, genuine.

Dirty - Bad, when applied to weather.

Division - Electoral district, equivalent to constituency in UK.

Dob - To inform on. To "dob (somebody) in" is to inform on somebody.
Docket - A bill, receipt.
Doco – Documentary.
Doona - British duvet. From the brand name Doona.
Drongo - Foolish person.
Drum - Information, tip-off ("I'll give you the drum.").
Duchess – Sideboard.
Duck's nuts, duck's guts or bee's knees - Something that is perfectly suited.
Dummy - A device, usually plastic, for babies to suck. cf. American pacifier.
Dummy, spit the - Get very upset at something.
Dunny – Toilet.
Dux - Top of the class (n.); to be top of the class (v.).

E

Earbashing - Nagging, non-stop chatter.
Emu bob - The duty given to enlisted men in the military, of picking up cigarette butts lying around barracks and parade grounds.

F

Fair dinkum - True, genuine; see dinkum.
Fair enough - I don't see a problem with that; OK.
Fair go or fair crack of the whip - A chance or a reasonable opportunity to complete a task.
Fair shake of the sauce bottle - A request to cut the speaker some slack, used as a preface to a statement.
Fair suck of the sav - Exclamation of wonder, awe, disbelief.
FBT - A large truck, "fucking big truck."
Feral - A derogatory term for variety of modern day "white-trash."
Flat chat, flat out - Moving as fast as possible; hence, busy.
Flick - To "give (something or somebody) the flick" is to get rid of it or him/her.
Flog - To sell something or to steal something or

to treat something roughly.

Fly wire - Gauze flyscreen covering a window or doorway.

Footpath - Any well-used walkway.

Fossick - To prospect, for example for gold; hence to search, to rummage.

Franger – Condom.

Fremantle doctor - The cooling afternoon breeze that arrives in Perth from the direction of Freeo.

Fuck truck - A panel van fitted out with mattress in the back for amorous liaisons.

Fugly - Fucking ugly.

Furphy - False or unreliable rumour.

G

Garn - Go on; going; for example "Garn y'mongrel."; see carn.

Ganda or gander - To take a look at something.

G'day - Dood day, hello.

Give it a burl - Try it, have a go.

Gobful, give a - To abuse, usually justifiably.

Gobsmacked - Surprised, astounded.

Going off - Used of a night spot or party that is a lot of fun.

Good oil - Useful information, a good idea, the truth.

Good onya - Good for you, well done.

Goon - Cheap cask wine.

Gun - Of excellent ability.

H

Hang shit - To mock, sully, denigrate, slander; to "pay out."

Hills Hoist - A type of rotary clothes-line.

Heaps - A lot; very. To "give someone heaps" is to pour mockery and/or abuse on them.

Heaps good - South Australian term to mean "very good".

Hooly dooley - A term used when something out of the ordinary happens.

Hoon - To drive fast, loudly, and irresponsibly.

Hooroo – Goodbye.

Hottie - Hot water bottle.

How ya gahn - How have you been/how are you doing.

Humpy - Small Aboriginal shelter, or any temporary outdoor shelter.

I

Idiot box - A television set.

J

Jet - To go somewhere in a hurry.

Jaded - Feeling hungover or suffering the after effects of drugs.

K

Kangaroos loose in the top paddock - Intellectually inadequate.

Kenoath - Contraction of "fucking oath."

Kero – Kerosene.

Kick on - Partying on after a discotheque or night club has finished.

Kindie – Kindergarten.

Knackered - Tired, exhausted.

Knock - To criticise

Knock back - (noun) Refusal, (transitive verb) Refuse

Knock up - Make pregnant (from the U.S.) or wake up in the morning (from the U.K.) or hit on the side (or back) of the head

L

Lend of, to have a - To take advantage of somebody's gullibility.

Light globe - An incandescent light bulb.

Lingo - Language or dialect.

Lippy – Lipstick.

Lob or lob in - Drop in to see someone.

London to a brick - Absolute certainty for example "It's London to a brick that taxes won't go down."

Long paddock - The side of the road where livestock is grazed during droughts.

Lunch box, open one's - To fart.

Lurk - Illegal or underhanded racket.

M

Manchester - Household linen.

Mangkin - A common, often Western Australian expression used to describe the behaviour of someone on drugs.

Mate's rate or mate's discount - Cheaper than usual for a friend.

Matilda - Swagman's bedding, sleeping roll.

Metho - Methylated spirits.

Mickey Mouse - Excellent, very good; inconsequential.

Milk bar - A shop where milk-shakes and other refreshments can be bought.

Moll - Used to describe a person or persons who have perpetrated an act, spoken words, or generally just 'done something' to annoy the user of this word.

Mozz or to put the mozz on – Jinx.

Mungin' - To eat veraciously; to perform oral sex.

Munted - Either broken, mangled or state of inebriation.

Muntyhead - One who likes to get munted.

Muster - Round up sheep or cattle.

N

Nah - No. "nah, im too busy."

Natio – Nationality.

Nasho - National Service (compulsory military service).

Nature strip (or verge in Western Australia) - A lawn or plantation in the road reserve between the property boundary and the street.

No drama - Same as no worries.

No sweat - Same as no worries.

No worries or nurries - You're welcome; no problem.

Nong (or ning-nong) - An idiot.

Noon - As opposed to the British English midday.

Norgs – Breasts.

Not the full quid - Not bright intellectually.

No wuckin' furries - A spoonerism of no fuckin' worries, has the same usage as no worries.

Nut out - Hammer out; work out.

O

Occy strap - Elastic strap with hooks on the ends for securing items.

Okey-dokey – OK.

On ya bike - As in "get on your bike."

Onya - A congratulatory term.

Op shop - Opportunity shop, thrift store, place where second hand goods are sold.

P

Paddock - See 'long paddock.'

Paro/parro – Drunk.

Pearler - An excellent example of something.

Perv - Short for pervert.

Pez - Something of poor value or perceived to be less worthy than others.

Piece of piss - Easy task.

Pig's arse - I don't agree with you.

Pinged - Caught doing something wrong.

Pink slip, get the - Get fired.

Piss – Beer.

Pissed – Drunk.

Pissed off - Angry.

Pissing into the wind - Futile efforts.

Piss in the woods - Simple, easy.

Piss-fart around - To waste time.

Piss off - To get lost; to leave.

Piss-weak or piss-poor - Weak; ineffectual; pathetic; unfair: a general purpose negative.

Pissing down - Raining heavy.

Pissing myself laughing - To be greatly amused. figurative.

Pokies - Poker machines, fruit machines, gambling slot machines.

Poof, poofter – Homosexual, derog.

Poofteenth - A minuscule amount, a smidgen.

Porcelain bus, driving the – Vomiting into a toilet.

Porker - A lie, "he's tellin porkers" or "its just porkers."

Port - Any form of hand luggage.

Pov or povo - Cheap looking; from poverty.

Pozzy – Position.

Preggers, preggo – pregnant.

Prezzy - Present, gift.

Q

Quack - A doctor. "I have to visit the quack."

Quid, make a - Earn a living.

Quid, not the full - Of low IQ; quid is slang for a pound, £1 became $2 when Australia converted to decimal currency.

R

Rack off - Push off! get lost! get out of here! also "rack off hairy legs!".

Rage – Party.

Rage on - To continue partying - "we raged on until 3am."

Rapt - Pleased, delighted.

Ratshit - Broken, not working properly; extremely drunk.

Reckon - You bet, absolutely or giving your opinion.

Rego - Vehicle registration.

Ridgy-didge - Original, genuine.

Righto - Okay or that's right. Can also be said as rightio.

Right, that'd be - Accepting bad news as inevitable.

Rip snorter - Great, fantastic, excellent.

Ripper - Something that is excellent, great, fantastic; similar to beauty.

Rock up - To turn up, to arrive.

Root - Slang term for sex.

Ropeable - Very angry.

Rort - Cheating, fiddling, defrauding.

Rough as guts - Rough, bumpy, of poor quality.

Rubbish - To criticise.

S

Satched - To be extremely wet.

Scab - To take something with no direct recompense.

Scrag - An unattractive woman.

Scrag fight - A fight between two women, usually physical.

Scratchy - Instant lottery ticket.

Sealed road - A road covered in bitumen.

Servo - Service station (i.e. petrol station / gas station).

Sheila - Woman.

She'll be right - It will be okay.

Sheltershed, lunch shed, weather shed or undercover area - In most States a simple detached building for the protection of school children from hostile weather.

Sherbet - Beer. As in "going to to the pub for a couple of sherbets."

Shirty - Polite version of shitty or pissed off.

Shitfaced - Inebriated.

Shit-hot - Exclamation, excellent.

Shout - To treat someone or to pay for something, especially a round of drinks.

Showbag - Full of shit.

Shower in a can – Deodorant.

Shonky - Poorly made, of low quality; dishonest, dubious, underhanded.

Shoot through - To leave.

Shot - Abandoning some venture one has become sick of.

Shotgun - Derivative of 'bags', used to claim ownership.

Sick - Very good.

Sickie - A day of absence from work, sometimes due to feigned illness.

Skite - Boast, brag.

Slapper - Easy or loose female.

Slaughtered - Either extremely tired or drunk.

Sledge - To insult members of the opposing team in a sports match.

Sleepout - House veranda converted to a bedroom.

Slurry - A promiscuous young woman, similar to slut or skank.

Spare - Very angry or upset.

Spew – Vomit.

Spewin – Angry or disappointed.

Spiffy, pretty spiffy - Great, excellent.
Spit the dummy - Get very upset at something.
Spruik - To promote or sell something; cf. British flog.
Sprung - Caught doing something wrong.
Squiz - A look, as in "Take a squiz at the new house."
Standover - Using intimidation or threat of violence to coerce others.
Station - A big farm/grazing property.
Steak - A story irrelevant to the current line of conversation.
Stella - Good, pleasing, thanks.
Sticking out like dog's balls - Very obvious.
Stickybeak - To nose around.
Stoked - Very pleased.
Strewth! - Exclamation, mild oath.
Strike! - Exclamation.
Stuffed - Exhausted, tired.
Stuffed, I'll be - Expression of surprise.
Stung - Hung over; disappointed.
Sunbake – Sunbathe.

Super - Short for superannuation, the Australian term for a private retirement pension, equates to the US 401k.
Suss - Suspicious; suspect or to figure something out.
Swag - Soiled up bedding etc.
Sweet - Fine, good.

T

Ta - Thank you.
Take the piss - Taking fun of.
Tall poppy syndrome - The attitude taken by common people of resenting those who, due to social, political or economic reasons act egotistical and flaunt their success without humility.
Technicolour yawn, to have a - To vomit.
Tee-up - To set up (an appointment).
Tickets, to have on oneself - To have a high opinion of oneself.
Tight - Thrifty with money.

Tinny - Small aluminium boat, a can of beer.

Tinny, tin-arsed – Lucky.

Tits on a bull, as useful as - Something completely useless.

Toey - On edge, nervous, distracted; horny.

Togs – Swimming costume, bathers

Too right - Definitely; that is correct.

Troppo, gone - To have escaped to a state of tropical madness.

True blue - Completely loyal to a person or belief.

Turps - Turpentine, alcoholic drink.

Two up - A gambling game played by flipping two coins simultaneously.

U

U-ey (chuck a U-ey, hang a U-ey) - Perform a U-turn in a vehicle.

Un-Australian - Considered to be an example of unacceptable behaviour or policy in Australia.

Unco - Clumsy, uncoordinated.

Uni – University.

Unit - Flat, apartment.

Up oneself - Have a high opinion of oneself.

Up somebody, get - To rebuke somebody.

Up the duff - Pregnant (i.e., my sheila's up the duff).

V

Veg out - Relax in front of the TV.

W

Wag - To skip school or work.

Walkabout - Meaning to take a journey of significant duration with no specific destination.

Wing - To pass, to give; to undertake a task.

What do you think this is, bush week? - Disbelieving response to some one you think is trying to con you.

Whatever you reckon - A dismissive to indicate

that a person is lying or
talking rubbish.
Whinge - Complain;
similar to crying, but
more commonly used for
adults.
Whiteant - To criticise
something to deter
somebody from buying
it.
**Wrap one's laughing
gear** - To eat something.
Wobbly - Excitable
behaviour.
Wog - Flu or trivial
illness.

Y

Yabber - Talk (a lot).
Yakka – Hard work.
Yarn - To talk.
Yeah-no/yeah-nah - Non-
committal expression
with various
applications.

A Note on Sources

Much of the information in this book was culled from our own knowledge of British English. We did countless hours of research watching British TV and writing down words and phrases. We also drew on several sources, including Wikipedia, Wiktionary and countless other freely available sources on the web. We wanted to make this dictionary as comprehensive as possible, so our lists of words are made up from multiple sources combined into one master list we developed on our own. We have also used words that we've learned while on our many travels throughout Britain. For the updated second edition we also added hundreds of words that were suggested to us by readers of Anglotopia and this book. Thank you for all the contributions!

Also, many thanks must be given to John Rabon, who wrote some of the articles towards the end of the book and has consented to their use in this book.

And finally, thanks to Laurence Brown for his diligent copy editing.

ABOUT THE AUTHOR

Jonathan Thomas is the founder of Anglotopia.net -
the website and magazine for people who love
Britain. He's a passionate Anglophile who loves
everything British. Jonathan and his wife Jackie travel
to Britain often for both research and pleasure. His
dream is to one day make his home in Dorset with his
beautiful wife Jackie and two lovely children.